To the
persistent prayer
nucleus
in
Wales

To BRYN . . . who believed so earnestly that
God wanted to say it through me . . .

To Bryn's wife EDNA . . . who prayed I'd
believe him . . .

To Bryn's brother KERI . . . who prayed the
book into being . . .

To Keri's dear wife CAROL . . . who prayed
with him . . .

And to
GENE . . . who encouraged me always . . .

If you see Lennie...

by Char Potterbaum

Whitaker House

504 LAUREL DRIVE
MONROEVILLE, PA 15146

© 1974 by Whitaker House
Printed in the United States of America

International Standard Book Number:
0-88368-034-3

Whitaker House
504 Laurel Drive
Monroeville, Pennsylvania 15146
(412) 372-6420

LETTER ONE

I can see her yet. Young, zany, fun-loving Lennie. Her real name was Lenore, and as I recall, her husband's name was Les. But to know Lenore was to call her Lennie—because of the affectionate ring it has, I suppose. And so many years have slipped by I've forgotten her last name! But I remember our parting words to one another.

She said, "Char, I'm a lousy correspondent. I hate writing letters! How will we keep in touch?"

"Lennie, love knows no boundaries. Besides, you can always send up smoke signals if you need me!" (Twice she'd almost burned the house down melting bacon grease.)

And so, Lennie moved to the East.

All that remained of our relationship were fond memories of merriment shared and hearts laid bare and the empty house to the west of my kitchen window.

Losing touch with Lennie has been a real source of hurt to me. I have no one to blame but myself. I was so busy with the complicated business called marriage—you know—learning, rearing, adapting, mating, rebelling, submitting, rebelling, discovering, failing, cajoling, rebelling, pleading, heeding, needing—otherwise known as the school of hard "knots."

But praise the Lord! Somewhere just before Lennie came, I met Jesus. I discovered He was just the One for untying those hard "knots" of our experiences. And how I praise the Lord that I had the courage to share my Jesus with Lennie.

Lennie wasn't exactly the Jesus-embracing type. At first glance, you'd think of her as a real swinger. She was suave, sophisticated, very sexy (to use the vernacular) when she was with her socialite friends.

But when she was with me, she was just "Lennie" —warm, humorous, entertaining Lennie—and very much aware of a void in her life that was clamoring for Jesus, since her life was filled with problems just as mine was.

I presented her with a kind of "now and then" Gospel . . . as though some of the things Jesus did were still for "now," like salvation and comforting. But I must have left her with the impression that more tangible things, like healing and deliverance were just for "then."

I told her of a God who wanted to make her life abundantly rich and meaningful—when my own Christian experience was so meager and fruitless. I said Christ was a victor, when I knew deep inside I didn't have the victory over some despicable areas in my own life. I said He could make her joyful,

8

when the beginnings of a heavy depression were already forming deep inside me.

I told her that God wanted to bless us in a land that was flowing with milk and honey, and yet all she ever saw in my life was a brittle piece of manna that wasn't even strong enough to take away the odor of the garlic and onions of Egypt!

Well, human wisdom says there is "no use crying over spilled milk." Ah, but the blessed Holy Spirit says there is great merit in weeping over Lennie.

You see, He knows where she is. He knows what her needs are. And so He weeps for her through me.

For Lennie has come to mean more than "just Lennie" to me and to the Lord. She is the personification of all of the wives and mothers who have very real problems all over the world.

In Matthew 9:36 we read, "When He saw the throngs, He was moved with pity and sympathy for them, because they were bewildered—harassed and distressed and dejected and helpless . . ." (Amplified Bible).

To do a bit of paraphrasing "according to Charlene," we could easily translate that, "When He saw the throngs of bewildered *housewives*, He was moved with pity . . ." etc.

And so I have written this for the bewildered—who cry into their pillows at night (as I once did); the harassed who feel their husbands love their businesses more than they do their wives (as I once did); the distressed who cannot cope with life's simplest problems (as I could not); the dejected who have seemingly no place to turn.

And so, dear friend . . . these letters are for you. I have poured my heart out to Lennie because she was so easy to talk with, but nothing could please Lennie and me more than your peeking over our shoulders and sharing some mirth—and, I hope, some "worth" with us. I make no apologies for the seemingly ridiculous things that I have included, just as I do not try to explain my erratic behavior before my friends—who, like Lennie, accept me the way I am.

Oh! Praise God! It just came to me! Gill—Lennie Gill—that's her name! Oh, *if you see Lennie Gill, tell her I love her! And that Jesus loves her, too!*

LETTER TWO

Dear Lennie,

If you were still to the "west of my kitchen window," I'd do like we used to do. I'd wait 'til you came out to chain up the dog, then I'd push back the curtain and hold the coffee pot up to the window and nod my head furiously up and down. And, depending upon which way your head nodded back, I'd either plug the pot in or head over your way.

Lennie, those were good times. I really enjoyed them so much . . .

But now that you are gone, I can only stare back at the crazy reflection I see in my coffee pot and wish you were here.

Don't misunderstand me. I've known some great neighbors since you left. But there was only one Lennie . . . one special pair of twinkly blue eyes that could bring out the "goofy" streak in me like no other pair of eyes could.

Remember that coffee pot, Lennie? I bought it because you used to say, "Got time for a cup of coffee?" and I'd say, "Sure—it'll only take an 'instant,'" and the look of horror on your face told me I'd better get with the real thing.

That original coffee pot has since been recycled somewhere in the great burying "grounds" beyond . . . and several others have replaced it. But each new coffee pot always reminds me of me—a bit thick through the middle and a little heavier on the bottom, holding one arm to the side to ward off mild fits of hysteria, and the other one raised to heaven for good measure.

Lennie, I found I was just like that coffee pot in another way. I needed to be plugged into some mainstream of power to cause the Living Water within me to bubble and surge and become something other than stagnant and unmoving. I needed some power to force that Living Water through my innermost being so that all the Bible knowledge I had stored away in my "top basket" could seep down into the depths of me where He could use it to quench the thirst of others. I needed to learn the value of being controlled by Someone greater than I, so I could be "poured out" to others.

Lennie, it was a dynamic encounter with the Holy Spirit that has made my earlier experience with Jesus become "flavorful." It was His power flowing through me that caused me to wake up to the needs of others around me.

Oh, Lennie—so many years have gone by. And if I were to tell you that they were all "good" years, no doubt my halo would come clattering down around my wire rims! They were good in that God's purpose was being worked out in my life—but they were "bad" from a human standpoint because of my inability to walk in victory.

And as I look back now, I realize that my circumstances were really not all that bad. It was my rotten attitude *toward* those circumstances that brought such misery into my life and into the lives of those around me. It took me years to learn that victory could be mine if I would accept things as they were and learn to "thank God in everything —no matter what the circumstances" were (I Thessalonians 5:18 Amp.).

And so, the only way to catch you up on all that has been happening in our lives is to start at the beginning. And yet, where is the beginning? For it all began in the heart of God even before the beginning of time, according to Romans 8:29. It says, "for those whom He foreknew—of whom He was aware and loved beforehand—He also destined from the beginning (fore-ordaining them) to be molded into the image of His Son (and share inwardly His likeness) . . ." (Amp.).

He foreknew that I would be born to a specific set of parents, having formed within me all the attributes, both good and bad, of preceding generations.

He set me continually in just the right circumstances that would bring about a need for a conversion experience early in my teens . . . again, circumstances that were "right" according to His working—not in the eyes of man, for Dad, as you

13

might remember, was a heavy drinker. He was too poor to be called an alcoholic—but my memory of him is too tender ever to call him a drunk. Lennie, he accepted Christ seven days before he died.

Through my own willfulness, the conversion experience became a blur as I grew into late teenage years being very aware of myself, and particularly aware of a deep need for love—a need that a doctor was later to tell me "could never be satisfied."

The Lord lovingly arranged for the boy of my dreams to be situated in my biology class so that he could intercept my mooney-eyed glances. This boy dated me and finally decided that it would take a lifetime to figure me out anyhow, so he might as well marry me.

Of course, that's Gene—your favorite "car starter" in zero degree weather when you'd throw up your hands in despair and motion for him to come and help.

How I praise the Lord for reserving Gene for me because He gave him to me when I didn't even know you were supposed to pray about such things. And I praise God for giving Gene a "tolerance level" far above most people's as he's stood by me through thick and thin—and heavy too. (My waistline has always been as unpredictable as my temperament.) I've been stretched out of shape by six pregnancies, all weighing somewhere between the nine and ten pound mark, and—Lennie? Did you faint dead away?

I guess it is a bit of a shock, isn't it? To think of

me—the typical, neurotically distraught housewife mothering six when I was having such trouble coping with three when you and I were neighbors. But I always tried to tell you I was completely irresistible, and you never believed me!

So now, on with the business of catching up. I'll be prattling on about people you don't even know. Don't let that bother you, because the thread I want you to see is the one you will see strung through all the letters. A deep, scarlet thread—blood-red and strong. It is the power of God, the activity of the Holy Spirit moving in and through circumstances, pushing obstacles aside, making the hard places smooth and the crooked places straight.

I don't even know if it's necessary to trip some lever in your memory bank as to my conversion and details involving it. I'd accepted Christ as a teen-ager, but turned my back on Him. And then one day, just a year or so before you moved by us, I became aware of an emptiness, a vacuum that needed to be filled. It was the place where Christ had once reigned in my life, and He wanted to take up residency there, again. He'd stayed quietly in the background, giving me no trouble—until He knew the time was right. And then, from the depths of my being I cried, "I need God!"

I was by myself in the living room. I cried like a baby and ran for an old, yellowed Bible I'd remembered seeing up in the attic. And my life has never been the same.

But so much has happened since you left, it

would take umpteen coffee breaks to ever catch up!

But now it's time for all the troops to come marching in; so I'd better go prepare for my three o'clock trauma. I drink two cups of terribly strong coffee, pray in the Spirit for fifteen minutes, then brace myself flat against the kitchen wall to give them a wide berth to the refrigerator, and wait breathlessly for the screech of the school bus brakes. Works every time!

More later,
Char

LETTER THREE

Dear Lennie,

Gene is still in the appliance business. He doesn't have the small store anymore. He always said, "In business, you have to think big," so he moved to another location when growing pains brought on by "thinking big" set in.

And I, not wanting to think anything less than "big" about the business I happened to be in (better known as child rearing) promptly had those six kids—and gained twenty pounds somewhere in the endeavor.

I was in Gene's store the other day, and someone mistook me for a saleslady. She said, "Do you have trash mashers?"

I said, "Oh, my yes. Six of them. They stomp on everything in sight and mash gooey things into the carpet every chance they get!"

My number two son, Don—you remember him —came to the customer's rescue and gently said, "Mother, please. Go. clean out the bathroom— again. I'll handle the customers."

I'm sure it seems quite impossible to you that

he could be old enough to manage the store, but an able manager he is, and old enough at that, as he and Larry are both in their early twenties now.

I guess this would be as good a time as any to give you a quick run-down on the kids. I hope it doesn't give you the same feeling I get when some doting grandmother in the doctor's office says, "Would you like to see my grandchildren?" as she flips out an endless plastic-protected panorama with like endless monologue.

Larry, number one son, is just out of the Army. I guess I'd have to say he is a part of the "new morality." Larry and I don't always see eye-to-eye—but that could be because he stands six-foot-four, and I always find myself trying to communicate somewhere in the area of his tie tack.

As I mentioned, Don works in the store. I hate to see him have all the long hours that Gene had, but he looks pretty healthy as though it agrees with him.

Do you remember when he and your Cindy pulled out Mrs. Mahoney's prize calla lilies? He says he doesn't remember Cindy at all. Seems strange when they were so inseparable at five.

Jan is in her very late teens. She is starry-eyed and in love. She must have been only about three when you moved away. That was when she would go around singing, "So let the sunshine in—face it with a grin—mothers never lose—and fathers never win, etc." She finally learned it right just before she started school.

Well, of course Laurie would be entirely fresh to you. Praise God, Laurie is always "fresh." Submissive, obedient—all the things that a daughter should be, as is Jan. She just barely squeaked into her teens, and she blushes occasionally because I won't let her go play touch football with certain boys when they call because their voices are changing.

Mark is full of energy—exuberant, spontaneous, ten-year-old energy.

Jamie? Jamie is the youngest—six—and a miniature Don. And, like Don, he is full of natural musical ability that amazes us.

There are no two of them alike. They are all precious to me, even with their varied temperaments and talents. I'm fishing around for things I can say that will not give away the fact that my heart nearly bursts with pride because of them. But they are all quite nice looking. Noses all centered neatly between both eyes—eyes that are all brown but for Mark's deep, mysterious blue ones.

Top all this off with a tremendously young-looking father who hasn't gained an ounce or aged one bit through all this rigorous ordeal known as bread-winning, and you come up with one fantastic family.

As for myself, I have changed in ways. I've come up through depression, nervous breakdown, insecurity, frustration—to finally become an example of what God can do when a person turns the reins over to Him.

Lennie, I'm not here to talk about diaper rash and recipes. I want to tell you a fantastic "something wonderful" about a Holy God Who cares—Who has cemented this whole sticky business of love and marriage and rocky beginnings into a monument to Himself!

And please don't expect me to be always coherent! This same Jesus I told you about tumbles miracles and happenings into our lives so quickly, I barely have time to finish one "hallelujah" before another is right behind it! We've learned to praise Him for everything—yes, even the bills that come in. I mean—after all, how else are you going to know if the mailman has come?

More later,
Char

LETTER FOUR

Dear Lennie,

When Lazurus was raised from the dead, I know he was thrilled with his new life. But until someone set him free from those grave-clothes he couldn't function properly. When the Lord commanded, "Loose him, and let him go," he was no longer restricted by his bonds.

Lennie, this letter might depress you a bit as bondage is never pleasant to dwell upon. But I feel the loveliness of Christ will shine forth more in later letters if you catch a glimpse of the ugliness of my "grave-clothes."

After you moved away, something began to settle over me that I'll refer to as The Great Depression. It didn't happen all at once. It was more like a creeping paralysis—subtle and cunning. Like living a lie. I would tell people that Christ could make them joyful, but I could give less and less evidence to it in my own life.

Although I couldn't have explained it then, I realize now that somewhere back in the caverns of my mind I gave in to a "thought" of depression.

I permitted it to take root. I became more concerned with circumstances that were foaming about my feet than with the Christ Who could lift me above them.

Those circumstances seemed so insurmountable. Gene's business, due to rapid growth, kept him away from home more and more. I found myself facing more responsibility than I cared to, and facing it alone. He'd taken on a leasing end of the business that necessitated his being out of town many days at a time. His business became my rival—much like another woman in my life. And sometimes, when I'd cry into my pillow, I'd think, "I could scratch another woman's eyes out—but the business? It's both my friend and my enemy, because it clothes and feeds me, and yet it robs me of Gene."

Without realizing it, I became more or less a chronic complainer. This only tended to throw Gene into business more than ever, because in his business he "felt adequate." I made him feel miserably inadequate by my continual stream of tears and quiet moods.

And too, I read the wrong kind of books. Nothing off-color, mind you—just books that spoke the wrong thing to my heart. Books that said our marriage couldn't survive under these circumstances. And, of course, I believed them. This negative attitude marched right into place beside the negative confession of depression, and the two began to work hand in hand.

Then well-meaning friends would come by and say, "My, I'd hate to be alone so much of the time like you are." They'd say, "If I were you, I'd make my husband shape up or ship out! I wouldn't put up with his being gone so much." (It's strange how they could never find chapter and verse to back their "wisdom" up.)

Self-pity now lined up with the other two trouble makers already on the scene.

I look back now and realize Gene was only doing what he felt was absolutely necessary—providing in the way *he'd* chosen for those things he felt I wanted. I'm sure he thought material "things" would help to combat the depression he was trying desperately not to notice.

Gene was like that, then. Rather than face an issue, he'd developed a keen knack for thinking, "If I ignore the problem, it just might go away." (And, from our experiences in marriage counseling, I think most men are like that.)

I guess the malady could best be described as "my-husband-loves-his-business-more-than-he-does-me."

Needless to say, we began to have a communication gap. The wider the gap became, the more hostilities rushed in to fill that gap. Hostilities are vicious things. Each hostility was like a throbbing hammer, making the wedge deeper, wider.

Lennie, "communication" is so hard to define. But I'll give you my definition. I believe that communication can only be established when two hearts are willing to beat in harmony. And there is only one way that self-willed, warped hearts are *going* to beat as one—and that One Way is Jesus. Until two people are willing to see themselves in the light of God's Word—The Truth—communication will not be established. Only when they see themselves the way God sees them—as needy sinners needing a Savior—not only in a one-time experience, but on a daily, moment-by-moment confrontation with this Jesus as LORD of their lives—will they truly be able to communicate love and forgiveness.

Oh, we didn't have knock-down, drag-out fights or anything like that. Maybe we could have faced things more quickly if we had.

We just got so we didn't talk at all. I gave up remembering there could be more to a morning conversation than "where's my socks?" and "please pass the toast." I nursed the deep ache I had on the inside—the ache that came from needing to feel loved—the ache that I couldn't share with anyone. And, of course, because I didn't feel loved, my natural assumption was that Gene didn't love me for if he did, I would *feel* loved.

As he threw himself into his business, I threw myself more and more into church activities. Not into "spirituality," mind you, just "activity."

I hid myself in the Word of God a lot of the time. I had a hunger for it that seemed to be insatiable. But there was no evidence of *power* in my life.

But, as I said, it was easier to live a lie than to

walk in truth. So, when at church functions, I was wonderfully gay and "twittery." Comments like, "Be sure to invite Char—we'll have more fun that way" fed that monstrous craving for attention I had. I felt if I made them laugh and be happy, they would desire my company. But when the throngs of "laughing" people left, I had only the lonely ache to face again.

Gradually it became more difficult for me to function. I couldn't do my work. I couldn't cope with the children. I was unable to enter into conversations. I was withdrawing more and more into a shell. A feeling of hopelessness gripped me. Gene, out of deep concern for my condition, made arrangements for us both to go for counseling to a Christian psychology center out West.

And too, I kept seeing Gene as the one who needed to change. It never occurred to me that it was my own lack of power and joy that kept him from seeking a closer walk with the Lord. He was quite comfortable in his initial acceptance of Christ and thought complacency was enough for him. He had no desire to go on with the Lord—not if I was any example of the outcome.

Well, I told you it wasn't a pretty picture. More like a "modern painting" I'd say . . . because the picture can be found on almost any block, on any street.

But, Lennie! When the scraping and chipping began—we discovered there was something beautiful and of value beneath the lie I'd been living.

25

And I must tell you about it—love compels me to tell you about it—love for Christ—love for man —new love for myself—new understanding of myself—a new and different way of "being." I hope you are eager to hear. . . .

More later,
Char

LETTER FIVE

Dear Lennie,

Will wonders never cease? I, the attention-starved, ego-maniac of the past, just now turned down an opportunity to be on TV!

About a year ago I was invited to make marzipan candy on "Homemaker's Time." It was really quite an experience—especially since I got to do all the clowning around I wanted to.

You should have seen how excited and nervous I was. The night before my "big TV debut" I remarked to Don, "Honey, tomorrow's the big day! Mom's going on TV!"

I guess he'd gotten wind of some of the clowning I'd done at a ladies club recently. He turned to me and said, "Uh . . . Mom? Could you do me a favor?"

I said, "Sure, Don. What's up?"

"Well, could you use your maiden name . . . please?"

I tell you, that boy is crazy about me.

Well, the next day there I was in living color,

facing those hot, hot lights and that ominous-looking camera.

From somewhere in the dark I heard a dramatic voice declare, "You're on!"

And I can only remember thinking, "I wonder which is going to wear off first—my deodorant or my nerve pill!" as I waded into the marzipan dough that got gooier by the minute. At one point I told them that my yellow paste hadn't turned out to be a very true yellow, so the trouble was not in their set—but if it was, they could call Potterbaum's Service! (I thought the MC was going to pass out!)

But in spite of my blooper, they called and asked me to come back again this year.

Lennie, I didn't even have to pray about it. I just politely said, "No, thank you. I'll not be able to." I said it very calmly, hardly able to believe I'd turn down an opportunity to be "front and center."

It was a good feeling to know that the need for attention had been satisfied.

What I'm trying to say is that Jesus is changing me! Daily and hourly, He is changing me! Lennie, it's so relaxing to step into a bunch of people and not have to "win them over" by dazzling them with a lot of chatter they didn't want to hear in the first place.

I remember back when I seemed to be almost "driven" to make myself the center of attention, a wise man quietly said, "Char, when are you going to find out that you could be loved for yourself and not for all the entertaining you can do . . ."

But I didn't want to hear him. It was too much of a threat. My humor was my only safeguard—my only weapon.

But let me tell you how this newer, more vital relationship with Jesus came about.

You see, there was a time when I thought all of life's answers could be found in little multi-colored pills. A pill to relax me, a pill to stave off the appetite, a pill to give me energy, etc. I used to tell my friends that happiness was a nerve pill over Christmas vacation. (Gene used to tell people I sounded like a slot machine when I rolled over at night.)

But, Lennie, now I know that true happiness can only be found in Jesus.

Loving Him!
Sharing Him!
Knowing Him!
Trusting Him!

I can't fully explain why I couldn't realize this earlier in my Christian experience. As I said, the knowledge hadn't "perked" through my entire being enough to become satisfying. When you and I were neighbors, I hadn't yet been put into that mainstream of power I so needed.

I couldn't seem to find satisfaction in any area of my life. There was a restlessness—an underlying conviction that there was "something more."

I talked to pastors down through the years, trying to find help. They never quite seemed to know what to do about the deep longing I had to know Him better.

One kind shepherd even went so far as to lean back in his chair and say, "My dear, there must have been someone in your past who was very spiritual, and you are desiring to pattern your life after him."

I was crushed! I only longed to be more like Jesus—wasn't He enough to pattern my life after? I knew deep within me that my anxieties could in no way bring glory to Him—and I wanted so to be rid of them.

And yet, my feelings were so hard to explain to anyone.

Another well-meaning pastor upset me when I was trying to relate some of my needs to him by telling me that "he feared for me—that I was ripe for the 'tongues movement.'"

I was absolutely indignant. *I* felt I was ripe for a *breakdown,* and he comes up with nonsense like that! I felt such deep hurt that he couldn't sense my need—couldn't understand my yearning for a heart-to-heart rapport with someone—anyone.

I told him I was so hungry to talk about Jesus— so hungry for vital Christian fellowship. Not the Sunday School party situations where you dunk doughnuts and play games. I was sick to death of those! I meant where you could *really* lay your heart bare and talk about Jesus.

I remember trying to tell a pastor about what I'd been experiencing in prayer. He seemed a little uncomfortable and remarked that there are some things about your prayer life you don't share with anyone. That wasn't too satisfying.

And another pastor said (when I tried to tell him of prayer experiences), "It sounds like you are trying too hard—doing it yourself." But I didn't buy that either. (Please realize that in sixteen years you can go through a lot of pastors!)

The hardest thing to understand was my firm conviction that I should leave my church. I'm not sure I'd ever even heard of the charismatic movement (maybe somewhere in the back of my mind I knew about it from magazines I'd picked up), but as for my ever being a part of it—it was unthinkable. I'd been a "fundamentalist" for sixteen years!

Gene's attitude had always been "anything to keep her happy." But by the time that strummed across my heartstrings, it always came through as, "I don't care—do as you please," to the tune of indifference.

He wasn't all that interested in church anyhow. Why should he be? What had he seen in my life that would make him long for anything "deeper" than what he was experiencing? Business was much more rewarding for him. He "understood" his business. It was real and tangible. But a Christ professed, and not possessed, can be very unrealistic —handy for a topic, come Sunday morning, but

31

not enough to sink your teeth into during the week.

And so . . . we left the security of the denomination we'd been a part of for so many years. The last night we attended was on a night when the Easter cantata was being presented. I had the soprano solo. I sang the song "All My Life" by John Peterson. It is a song of dedication, and I poured my heart into it—because for me it was truly a song of dedication. I knew there had to be something more, that a step of faith was necessary, and that God would not fail me. A hunger for more of Christ was gripping me in a way I couldn't understand or explain to anyone else . . . I knew He had something in mind . . .

And God, the only One Who can fully understand the aching heart—the longing heart—having placed that longing there himself, began to make His arrangements. The step of faith had been taken. Now the rest was up to Him.

His answer came in just a matter of a few short weeks. But as is so often the case I didn't realize immediately that this *was* my answer.

At this time, a friend from a different denomination shared with me the glowing account of a guest speaker who had come to their church to give a vibrant testimony—the kind you couldn't forget.

She said it had something to do with the activity of the Holy Spirit in some strange areas such as deliverance, healing, supernatural happenings—

it all had an appealing ring to it, because it seemed as though this young man believed that miracles were for today—that if Jesus was "the same yesterday, today and forever," then His power should be the same—that it was our obvious lack of faith and mountainous unbelief that hindered the flow of His power—not Christ Himself.

He'd been holding prayer meetings weekly in a small town nearby. Several of my friends went off to investigate this "unusual" prayer meeting and came to drag me off to it the following week.

I know they had told me in passing that this movement had something to do with a strange phenomenon called "speaking in tongues," which our former church held in abhorrence. But God had completely wiped that out of my mind, knowing that I wouldn't go if I had even given that a second thought. Oh Lennie, I can't praise Him enough! His guidance has been so precious! His ways are past finding out!

Well, this is only the beginning of what seems like a spectacular dream. Sometimes I'm so afraid I'm going to wake up and find out this isn't all real—and when such thoughts creep in, He quickly comes to me and assures me that it is all real. His Presence is proof—His Word declares it—and I have the witness of His Spirit within me that "it is real!"

Oh, I've got so much to tell you—so much to tell! But if there is any one thing I have learned, I've learned that I can best prove my love for Him

by being the wife and mother He wants me to be—
so off to the unmade beds, the piles of laundry, to
hot chocolate cups that will probably have to be
pried up with a table knife because I've taken too
long here with you!

But God loves me immeasurably, Lennie! And
Gene loves me immeasurably! At long last, I can
KNOW it! And life is meaningful! Jesus has
MADE it so!

Sometimes when I think of the wonder of it all,
I get absolutely tipsy in the Spirit! Oh, I hate to
leave you here—but duty calls . . . I'll be back
as soon as I can.

Love,
Char

LETTER SIX

Dear Lennie,

When that trumpet sounds and the Lord takes us "up" to be with Him, I sure hope I'm not standing under the little boys' bedroom. I'd never make it "up" through all that debris! Lennie, if you see a saint floating heavenward with a giant-sized halo, be assured it's me—only that's Jamie's drumhead I'm wearing!

Said challenging room is my project for today, but I can squeeze just enough time in here before tackling the impossible and the arrival of the three o'clock masses to go on with my story.

I mentioned in the letter before that my friends came to "drag" me off to this unusual prayer meeting. Guess it doesn't give much illusion to tact and grace, but "drag" is still a good word, because they didn't give me time to change out of my slacks or even time to finish the cake I was baking. They mumbled something about it all being "very informal," and that no one there would care about finery—they were so intent on Jesus. I had some haphazard thoughts about what Gene might think,

35

but he was on a business trip and wouldn't be home until late in the night, anyhow—surely he wouldn't care. . . .

Lennie, the experience was absolutely indescribable. But I'm going to try to describe it anyhow. I'll tell you the way I tried to tell Gene. (He'd come home earlier than expected and was waiting for me.)

I started bubbling over about the prayer meeting while the incident was still fresh in my mind.

I said, "Honey, it was like a pep session for Christ, and—and a family reunion, all rolled into one! I could sense the Presence and Power of God just thick all over the place! And love—I never felt such love before!

To which he hardly even rattled his newspaper.

He heard me say something about kids on drugs getting straightened out, and that it was so crowded we all had to squeeze together on the floor, and he still didn't say too much.

Then I said, "And Gene, I heard someone speaking in tongues for the first time . . ."

"You heard WHAT?" The newspaper came down with a crunch. And the look on his face told me that I'd never get him to go with me, much less be allowed to go back myself. He may not have been a very interested "fundamentalist," but he'd picked up enough tales about "tongues" to be convinced that tongues were of the devil and his mind closed tighter than a pickle jar lid!

I was crushed.

36

How could he pass judgment on something he hadn't even witnessed? And oh, how that fellowship had caused my heart to yearn for what they had . . . how could he?

Couldn't he see my excitement? It was the first thing that had sparked life in me for months. I was still having problems with unnameable anxieties and fears even after the extensive therapy I received from the Christian Psychology Center out West. Somehow, like a wisp of hope in the back of my mind, I kept thinking, "This 'baptism of the Holy Spirit' business they keep talking about . . . could it be what I needed to live the radiant, vibrant kind of life that could truly exalt Christ?"

You should have been there, Lennie! Beautiful fresh-faced young people with arms uplifted whispering, "Jesus, I love You—praise Your Holy name! Glory to God . . ." And really meaning it, because I found out on the way home that many of them had been in the very depths of sin—that they loved Him much because they had been forgiven of so much.

The music was next to ethereal. Their guitars were tuned together, as were all their hearts in harmony with the One who had forgiven them. The Lord gives them melodies, then guides them as to which scripture to put the melody with, and poof! Just like that, they have a stirring song of praise. These bits of melody went deep down into my heart—deep where that ache was. And there was something so touching about actually using the Bible as the hymnbook.

Another thing—they laid their hearts bare. They had nothing to hide . . . they weren't wearing a mask like the rest of the world. They knew the meaning of "body ministry." They shared gems from the Word they'd discovered, then someone would say, "That's just what I needed. Thank you for ministering to me. . . ." Lennie, I sensed depth in what they were sharing. I knew it had something to do with "deep calling unto deep. . . ." But I couldn't fully understand it yet.

I couldn't stop crying. The blessing from God was so great—once I even tried to lift up my hands in worship as they did, but I discovered I was too inhibited—too "churched." So I had to be content with just lifting up my heart.

But I knew I couldn't rest until I'd gleaned every bit of information from the Word about the baptism in the Holy Spirit that I could. It was a cinch I wasn't about to ruffle the church fathers' feathers with such an idea. This had to be between the Lord and myself. I wiped my mind clean of anything I had ever been taught and searched the Word as though I'd never seen it before. This time, I allowed the Holy Spirit to teach me—and Him alone. No commentaries. No manuals. Just He and I walking through those pages, and I trusted His ability to lead me into the truth.

Several weeks went by.

Every Thursday I would go to Gene and ask, "May I go to the prayer meeting tonight?"

Always the reply was the same—an emphatic "No!"

But poor Gene hadn't reckoned on the praying power of this tremendous group so in tune with the Holy Spirit. They knew I wanted to come back, and were praying from their end that I might get permission. My other two friends were attending the meetings, and they kept me informed as to what was going on. Sometimes, even I found it hard to believe all their enthusiasm. I found myself thinking, "If only I could go to a second meeting—maybe it wasn't all as great as I remembered—they could be exaggerating."

Gene's saying no so often didn't upset me. I only asked once each week and then let it go without the usual pouting or temper tantrums. I was a bit amazed myself with my reaction to his repeated noes but Gene was being completely dumbfounded by my submission. (He told me later that every time he said no, my submissive attitude made him feel even more like a heel.)

Well, once upon a Thursday, Vic (the young school teacher who'd been having these meetings in his home—now our pastor) had promised his wife to pick up a dryer part that she needed. Our appliance store happened to be on his way home, so he stopped in and made himself known to Gene.

I guess Gene decided Vic looked all right—not

shifty-eyed or anything like that—so he let me go to the meeting that night.

Hallelujah!

And the timing was right, because I'd already made an appointment to go to the local psychology center for more help. Gene had seemed a bit crestfallen when I told him I had made the appointment, because it was sure to cost us a pretty penny.

But I *had* to have help. Those anxieties within me! They were frightening me! I seemed to be gripped by fears I couldn't put into words, and I could hardly cope with the simplest problems.

If I was asked to come up with a cake for P.T.A., I crumbled. If someone came in for a cup of coffee, I died a thousand deaths inside of me. There was a continual tightening in my throat that made me feel as though I were constantly being choked to death. I even imagined that my voice sounded squeaky at times because of this constriction. (The doctor said, "Just nerves.")

In all those weeks of searching I had come face to face with God. I was crying out to Him to give me some answers. Was this baptism in the Holy Spirit the link I needed to line up His power and my evident weakness into something usable?

I felt as though I were standing right in the middle of Romans 7, pleading for help. The things I wanted to do—exude joy, see a move of God in the lives of others, have patience with the kids, be rid of irritability—these things I couldn't see. Instead, I saw my own joylessness and no one being interested in my Savior (no matter how much or how long I talked to him). I was embarrassingly impatient with the kids.

As you can see, I needed help.

But so does the boys' bedroom, so I'm off to chase dust bunnies and remove bubble gum as "unto Him."

Back later . . .

Char

LETTER SEVEN

Dear Lennie,

Finally, after twenty-three years of sidestepping tinker toys and building blocks, Gene says I'm walking almost normally again. This is the first time in all those years I haven't had a preschooler around. Now the only thing on my daily obstacle course is an occasional car track or paper airplane.

When Jamie went strutting off in triumph and disappeared behind those school bus doors for the first time, I can't say it was really a tearful experience, his enthusiasm was so great. (I think watching him reject his teddy bear was harder on me.) Besides, I immediately stepped out from behind the lump in my throat and got busy with something I'd had in the back of my mind for years . . . writing! I only let enough time elapse to adjust to the quiet—and the clock ticking (I really couldn't remember having heard one tick in all those years) before I went out and bought a small typewriter and a b-i-i-g wastebasket.

I'm sure I shared my desire to write with you. I've wanted to write since I was an unrealistic young girl in high school. Now that I've faced reality, I feel the need to write even more keenly than before.

But while I'm waiting for something to sell, I'll keep tapping all this out to you. It gives me a good feeling all over again just to share these experiences —if only with a ticking clock and a clacking typewriter, because the experiences have been so fantastic.

Oh, Lennie—there is so much to tell—and keep telling and keep telling! There seems to be no end!

Take that second prayer meeting, for instance:

As I mentioned, I kept thinking maybe the first meeting had been played up too much in my own imagination . . . a second meeting might not be as great.

Lennie, it wasn't my imagination. "Where the Spirit of the Lord is there is liberty. . . ." And these lovable "fanatics" worshiped Him in liberty —not noisily or distastefully—but with liberty. I cried my way through the second meeting just as I had the first. I didn't really care whether anyone noticed or not. Besides, I wasn't the only one crying. Maybe that's why charismatics are known as emotional—because they have enough sense to cry when they feel the blessing of God in a meeting. And because they have enough sense to know that love is a pretty strong emotion and needs to be expressed.

Lennie, those people knew how to praise the Lord. I was still as inhibited as I had been at the first meeting, but I wasn't so inhibited that I couldn't look around at the faces uplifted to Him in un-self-conscious adoration, people with arms held high in a gesture of surrender.

I knew I no longer wanted to be on the outside looking in. I wanted what they had—I wanted to share their zeal, their depth—and most of all, I wanted the baptism of the Holy Spirit. I had searched the Scriptures daily and was convinced that it was a valid experience.

After the meeting I went up to Vic and began to ask him some typical questions such as, "I've been taught that I received the Holy Spirit when I was saved, that I got it all in one package."

He gave me his boyish grin and said, "In essence, that's right. But have you ever 'unwrapped' the package?"

I looked at him in amazement as he went on.

He turned to John 7:37. 'If any man thirst, let him come unto me and drink . . . He that believeth on me, as the Scripture hath said, out of his belly shall flow rivers of living water . . . But this spake He of the Spirit, which they that believe on Him should receive, for the Holy Ghost was not yet given. . . .'

"You see, Char . . . accepting Christ is like taking a drink of water . . . but to be baptized in the Holy Spirit is to have the rivers of living water flowing out from within you—to others. Do you see the difference?"

Desire must have been written all over my face

44

because longing for this experience was written all over my heart!

"Charlene, would you like to ask Jesus to be your Baptizer in the Holy Spirit tonight? Would you be willing to ask Him . . . in your own words . . . for the unfolding of this precious gift in your own life?"

Would I! Oh, how I wanted this . . . above everything else . . . above church membership . . . above social status . . . above family relationships. . . .

Vic directed me to a small room and asked Peg and Pam if they'd please come with us. I knelt down, and as they placed their hands upon my head, I asked Jesus to baptize me with His Holy Spirit, and I asked in faith believing.

Lennie, words are so inadequate. Even now, as I witness others asking for this gift I think "there are no words to describe what is going on within them right now." But every time I hear the song "Heaven came down and glory filled my soul," I am reminded of this treasured moment.

It seemed as though billows and billows of His love washed "clean" over my anxiety-trodden soul. All the fears—those unnameable fears that had plagued me so long—had to flee! His love literally chased them away! Oh, Lennie, I was FREE! Do you know what it's like to be free? Free to live— free to love—free to be yourself! Free to be quiet— free to worship without inhibitions? Free! . . .

As He sent His torrents of love through me, I

45

felt praise welling up from somewhere in the depths of me. That praise came forth in a beautiful, undeniably supernatural prayer language. As this praise came forth, my arms went heavenward without anyone's suggesting it. It was *my* gesture of love and self-surrender.

As I got up from my knees, I felt so full of love that I hugged every sister in sight. Yes, Lennie—I said "sister." Remember how I hated that term? I'd always thought of it as archaic. But when I got up from my knees, I realized that these *were* my sisters in Christ.

Well, there I stood—right in the middle of an experience labeled "forbidden" by my former denomination, my husband, and my friends. But I knew that "neither life nor death, nor principalities, nor powers, things present, nor things to come" could separate me from this love of God I was experiencing. I knew for a certainty that I would never need those nerve pills again. And I knew for a certainty that He had a plan for my life.

I suppose if someone were to say "describe your experience in one word," I would say PEACE. From that moment there was a core of peace deep within me that I gloried in. The tightness in my throat was gone. (I remember rubbing my neck the next day because I felt as though my neck must be sagging down around my shoulders. Every muscle was so relaxed.) And of course, I wanted to share the whole experience with Gene, but I must admit I felt some fear and trembling as to his reaction.

However along with this peace came REST. Gobs and gobs of rest. I knew now that my Jesus was sufficient for any problem, any obstacle, any mountain. And moving Gene would indeed be mountainous—he'd been so against the whole business.

But this is just the beginning of an endless chain of miracles that have come our way. Must leave you here now, so you can digest all I have told you. Besides, it's time for the mailman. He told me once that he could always tell a writer by his attachment to his mail box.

More later,
Char

LETTER EIGHT

Dear Lennie,

The things I want to tell you about are coming at me so thick and fast I can hardly keep up with them! You should see me—I jot things down on meat wrappers, grocery tapes, even Kleenexes. Then one of my kooky kids will come in and grab the Kleenex and holler, "Oops. Sorry, Mom. Just 'blew' that one!" and I have to rack my brain to remember what I remembered! But back to my story. . . .

I waited until three weeks had gone by before I shared my baptism of the Holy Spirit experience with Gene. I waited first, because I had to be sure it was not just some emotional experience that was going to wear off; and secondly, I didn't really know how to explain such a thing *to* him. But in that three weeks, the experience became more real to me than reality itself. The peace I spoke of became more pronounced. Nerve pills were a thing of the past. The Lord had put me right in the middle of a pleasant land that was flowing with milk

48

and honey, and even the giants in that land didn't seem to unnerve me. I felt as confident as Joshua did in *his* promised land.

I spent most of that three weeks peeling grapes and feasting on luscious things in the Word I seemed to have missed altogether when I was bumbling around in the wilderness.

Continually, I prayed, "Lord, give me wisdom to know when to share this with Gene."

It happened three weeks to the very day after I received the baptism.

I waited until we were all snuggled in bed under a comfortable blanket of darkness so he couldn't find anything to hit me with.

I know the Lord had many reasons for creating darkness, but I've always been convinced that one of the prime reasons was to have an atmosphere most fitting for husband-and-wife sharing. You can best speak heart to heart when you can't see eye to eye. (And if you *can't* see eye to eye, you'd *better* speak heart to heart!)

Well, there we were.

Just me, and Gene—and Jesus.

Remember my saying I'd made arrangements to go to the local psychology center? And that Gene had been concerned because of the expense? I knew this would be my wedge.

I cleared my throat and said, somewhat weakly, "Gene?"

"Uh-huh."

"Would you like to hear how the Holy Spirit saved you several thousand dollars?" (This actually raised him up on one elbow.)

"How who *what*?"

At least I was sure I had his undivided attention. He was a businessman from the word "save," and I'd found his soft spot.

I said, "I want to tell you how Jesus saved you a mint!"

And as he scratched his head in bewilderment, I began to tell him of what happened when I received the baptism of the Holy Spirit. I could feel the love of Jesus enfolding us both, and I had no qualms about sharing the entire experience with him.

What I hadn't realized was that Jesus, who always "doeth all things well," had been preparing his heart right along.

As I went further into my "testimony," Gene drew me closer to himself. He apologized for not being with me when I "received." I assured him it was all right—that all things work together for good—that I was so thrilled he was understanding. The fact that I now prayed in tongues didn't even throw him. He seemed to be awed by the whole story.

Then, I felt I had to confess something to him.

"Honey, I need to ask your forgiveness."

"Why?" he asked, with a certain amount of trepidation.

"Because—well—because for years I've felt you

50

loved your business more than you did me, and yet with my *mind,* I know you've loved me. I just never seemed to be able to feel it in my *heart.*"

I thought he seemed a bit relieved.

I went on. "Your business has always been like the other woman in my life. It's been both my enemy and my friend—it's clothed and fed me— and yet I always felt it robbed me and the kids of *you!*"

My heart really ached for him. I thought of all his endeavors to accumulate more "things" to bring me happiness, his feelings of inadequacy because I couldn't be convinced of his love.

"Gene, I want to ask your forgiveness, because now I know that the only kind of love that can *truly* satisfy the human heart is the love of God I've experienced in these past three weeks. And I know now that had you gotten down on your knees and loved me adoringly—even worshipfully—it still never would have satisfied my heart as the love of Christ has in these past days. . . ."

And with these words, a great burden seemed to roll off my darling husband's back. It landed right at the feet of Jesus, where it belonged. His feelings of inadequacy left, and he was free to be himself, to be loved for himself, and to love me in a new way!

Our hearts were knit together with that confession in a way they had never been before. For the first time, Gene saw something in my Christian experience that appealed to him.

51

We laugh together now, because of things he had been experiencing in that three weeks. He said he saw such a change in me, he honestly was worried—because he thought I'd found a new lover. (I guess in a way, I had.)

He said he sensed something different—contentment, no depression, a calm—he even noticed that it didn't make any difference whether I was the center of attention when we went some place. Jesus was giving me that "meek and gentle spirit, which is in the sight of God of great price." I Peter 3:4b KJV.

Well, I can honestly say that it was "of great price" in the sight of Gene also, because from that moment on a great hunger began to grow within him, because my obvious peace was real enough to make him want the same peace. He began coming to the prayer meetings, and it wasn't too long before he asked for the baptism of the Holy Spirit also.

Interestingly enough, Gene's experience was much different than mine. Just more proof of our uniqueness and God's originality. He received the baptism much less emotionally than I did, but it was not any less "real." His love for Christ is growing by leaps and bounds, and, to quote him, he says, "I've never been so excited about being a Christian in my whole life!" And he really means it.

Needless to say, our joy is complete for now we are really "one" in Christ. I'm embarrassed when

I remember all those selfish prayers I sent heavenward (before the baptism), pleading, "Oh, Lord, please make Gene more spiritual . . ." when my real need was to ask the Lord to do a work in me so that my love for Christ would have some meaning for Gene.

I praise God that even in our "infantism" He knows our needs.

Well, I must stir the chili, so I will leave you here to sort this all out in your mind. I told you we were excited! And just think, there is more. . . .

Love,
Char

LETTER NINE

Dear Lennie,

If my letters are ever published I should title them "blessings in a boot box." I keep tapping all this out to you, and since I don't know your address, I toss them into an adjacent boot box. If I didn't, they'd become paper airplanes before the day was over!

Back to the business of "catching up."

One morning about 10:00, I got a phone call. I think it was only a week after I told Gene about receiving the baptism in the Holy Spirit.

I couldn't believe what I was hearing.

On the other end of the line I heard Gwen's voice coldly relating to me that she was divorcing her husband—that because we had been friends for a long time she wanted me to know—but in no way did she want me to try to influence her, or to interfere.

I was stunned.

There had been no indication of a problem in their home. I could only cry out, "Why, Lord?"

as I pictured the three darling little ones that would be so cruelly affected by this rift. I knew her husband to be somewhat "bombastic" at times—he *did* have an unpredictable temperament —but she had always been one of those "marriage is for keeps" types.

I listened to her, trying to let it all register.

When she'd finished speaking, I said, "Gwen, if you decide you need me—*really* need me—I'll come. But not until you call."

Then I started praying as I had never prayed before. I didn't know all the circumstances about their problem but my Lord did—so I put that prayer language to use as I lifted them both to Him.

At four o'clock in the afternoon, I got another call. A broken-hearted Gwen was sobbing "Will you please come over? I need you."

I went to her, feeling more helpless and useless than I have ever felt in my life. They were not Christians. Once a few years ago, she had even said to me "Char, I love you, but don't ever come at me with your Bible. . . ." And I had promised her I wouldn't.

I pulled into their driveway.

Her husband, Ted, on whom she had just served the papers the day before, was in the yard with the children. He gave me one of the most hurt looks I have ever seen.

We filed silently into the house.

55

Tearfully, the three of us just sat there.

Finally, through body-wracking sobs Ted said, "I can't give them up! I can't give my wife and babies up! If she will just give me two more months, I know I can change!"

I took his hand in mine. His face was covered with tears and his chin was trembling very much like a little boy's. And as we cried together, I felt the love of God enfolding us all—as He is accustomed to doing when He is about to accomplish His purpose.

I said, "Ted, it wouldn't make any difference. At the end of two months, you would still be Ted. But there is hope—because God could give you a new nature, if only you'd let Him—because He just did it for us! I can't do anything about your particular situation, but let me tell you what God has done for us!"

And I started telling them what I just told you in the preceding letters.

What a discovery I made! I found that if you just lift up Jesus Christ—just as He says in His Word . . . "And I . . . If I be lifted up, will draw all men unto Myself." He does exactly that! *He draws them unto Himself.*

Lennie, I watched another miracle unfold. As I told them how God had put our relationship back together again and about being healed emotionally—a great hunger grew in their hearts for my Jesus.

The strangest thing is—I wasn't even aware of it!

I remember taking their hands, and praying that the Holy Spirit would step in and make them whole, that they would come to see their need for Christ—I'm not really sure what all I *did* pray—nor is it important. It wasn't the *words!* It was the power of the Holy Spirit working in their hearts to accomplish His purpose in their lives that was important.

After we prayed together, I did the strangest thing. I said, "I'm going now." Maybe that doesn't sound strange to you—and yet, knowing me the way you did, you are probably thinking, "any other time she would have said 'put another pot of coffee on, and we'll talk this thing out!'"

That's exactly why my saying I was leaving sounded strange. But this strong impression was there—that the work was done, that there was nothing more to do—that Jesus had done it all, and done it *His* way, and now I should "scoot."

The next day, I got a phone call from Ted. He was tearful again, but these were tears of joy and great relief. His sentences were broken by sobs, but he said, "God is working. . . . Everything is going to be O.K."

I learned later that after I left, God's Presence became real to them. The love they felt made honest sharing possible, and for the first time they were able to face their problems squarely.

So now you see why we get so excited. The Holy Spirit can move in just any old place, in just any situation and get the job done, in His age-old way—by *His* Spirit.

More later!
Char

LETTER TEN

Dearest Lennie,

My Lord knew that six kids and a well-organized house were absolutely incompatible, so He gave me six kids and a well-organized memory instead. I can tell you which bat is peeking out from under which sofa, what sock is draped over which chair rung, whose hair ribbon is on what bookshelf, and which guitar pick I last sucked up in the sweeper . . . and yet, in spite of my well-organized memory, I can't remember where you moved! So here I sit, tapping all this out to you and wondering what my friends would think if they knew about my writing all these letters—that will never get mailed—to a friend of the past I can't find.

The other day one of my kids walked by and spied the letters.

"Mom? What is this—a book, or somethin'?"

I looked as respectably thoughtful as I thought someone with a well-organized memory should look and said, "Why not?"

A book of letters? From the heart of an "unknown" to the heart of a "misplaced person"? With content like that, only God could get such a thing published.

Don't misunderstand me. I can be blissfully happy without ever getting a book published, because my happiness stems from knowing Christ and continually learning more about Him. But if sharing Christ over one cup of coffee can be so thrilling, think how thrilling it would be to share Christ with thousands . . . but, no—of course not. I mustn't let my imagination run wild . . . must get my imagination well-organized like my memory is, and bring every thought captive to the obedience of Christ. There is real safety in that.

Besides, I have had such hassles with Satan when just sharing Jesus on a one-to-one basis—I hate to think what he would put a person through who dared to proclaim the wonders of this "walk in the Spirit" to the whole world!

Take the incident about Gwen and Ted, for instance.

We were so thrilled to watch the Holy Spirit putting things right in their lives. They started attending the prayer meetings and publicly professed Christ as their Savior. The areas of contention were being healed over with understanding and prayer, and they had more of an insight into their own lives and problems because they were beginning to understand the Word of God—a book that had always been "closed" to them before.

Naturally, we began to share these things He was

doing in their lives with others. Wow, did I ever run into trouble here! I hadn't really counted on the Enemy of our souls caring as much as he did. I found that about the time I would start sharing with someone about what the Lord had done for Gwen and Ted, he (Satan or some one of his myriads of pesky antagonists under him) would start in with his attacks.

He'd say, "Why are you telling others? Trying to prove your own importance, maybe? Want them to think you are indispensable to the Lord—right? Getting a little glory in there for yourself—right?" And on and on he would go without letting up for a moment. He had me tongue-tied and stammering for a while.

I realized that pride *could* be a real stumbling block to the Lord's effectiveness in our lives. I knew there had been a certain exhilaration about telling others—and did it mean I was enjoying some of the glory? I was miserable!

But isn't it just like the Lord to come in like a cleansing flood where Satan has muddied everything up?

Well, I got a good firm hold on a scripture, and I threw it into Satan's face! His taunts were causing me to feel "guilty." And I knew a "guilty feeling" was synonomous with "condemnation."

The scripture I clung to was Romans 8:1. "There is therefore now *NO* condemnation to them which are in Christ Jesus. . . ." And I put it to work, immediately.

First, I had to do something. I realized that conviction and condemnation felt very much the same. For instance, if you have done something wrong, the beloved Holy Spirit comes along and causes you to "feel" bad about it. This is His way of keeping channels clear, and helping you to "walk" in the light, as He is in the Light. He is "convincing" (or convicting) you that you have sinned, and that you need to go to the Lord and ask forgiveness.

But if, after having asked forgiveness, Satan comes along and causes you to "feel" guilty about the same thing all over again, this is *condemnation*.

Well, I couldn't recall having brought this squarely before the Lord, and decided this was the first thing I should do.

I went to my favorite trysting place—the place where He and I meet—and poured my heart out to Him. I told Him something like this:

"Lord, I love You. There is a deep craving within me for more of You. It's a craving I can't even understand myself, but I know You know all about it because it wouldn't be there if You hadn't put it there! And, since it came from Your heart before it settled into mine, I know that craving for more of You is going to accomplish whatever You want it to, Lord. I know You didn't give me this craving because of my goodness, my abilities, or any great resourcefulness I might have. More than likely because You choose the 'weak and foolish things of this world' that no man may glory in what you accomplish. Lord, I'm telling You as simply as I know how—I love You—and I want to do Your will. I don't know how many knotholes You are going to have to pull me through to bring this about, but I'm willing. But Lord—You'll have to take me the way I am, and You will have to do the changing in me. You'll have to take me as I am—imperfections and all. Lord, without a doubt, pride is one of my imperfections—and my inferiorities are nothing more than pride turned inside out. And 'self-seeking' is probably just another reflection of pride. But what am I to do, Lord? Tell myself that I shouldn't make some attempt to serve You because I might become more filled with pride? Fail to attempt something rather than attempt and flop? That's just another layer of pride! Maybe even a *worse* kind of pride! Lord, here I am. A shapeless chunk of stone that needs to be chipped and buffed—but a lively stone, Lord—a lively stone that knows You well enough to know that You can lower the 'boom' in chastening Power whenever it's necessary. Now Lord, until You purge these imperfections out of me, we are both stuck with them because I'm all I have to offer! Now, take my pride and grind it out Your way—turn those inferiorities right side out so I can accept myself the way I am—the way You made me. And in the meantime—please tell Satan that my pride and my self-seeking are *Your* problem and not *his*—and that he will have to get his pesky hordes off my back, in the Name of Jesus!"

With that prayer, I got off my knees and if I remember correctly, I think I stuck my tongue out at the devil. I recognized him for what he was—the accuser of the brethren.

But it solved the problem. Whenever he would come at me with his attacks, I would point back to the place and the time where I asked the Lord's forgiveness, then I would quote, "If we confess our sins, he is faithful and just to forgive us our sins . . ." and he would turn on his heels every time, livid with rage.

It's a good thing I learned how to deal with Satan, because he'd have had me completely defeated before the battle even got thick, if I'd listened to him.

But now I have to probe around in my well-organized memory to find out where in this unorganized house my seldom-organized son left his bike lock key.

Whatever do well-organized people who have well-organized children do with all their well-organized time?

More later.

Char

LETTER ELEVEN

Dear Lennie,

I can't praise the Lord enough for His protective care. A few weeks ago, Don was on a ten-foot scaffold working, and he fell completely to the ground along with a huge heater and the other fellow on the scaffold. Don didn't even get a black and blue mark! The heater was a little worse for the wear, and the other fellow had a broken ankle and two broken vertebrae. I was so grateful that Don wasn't hurt. I prayed, "Lord, thank You, but in my prayers I had included the other fellow, too. . . . Why, Lord?"

It was soon obvious. By being hospitalized and bedridden and crutch-dependent for a number of weeks, he and his wife had time to get re-acquainted, and they had a new chance to realize how much they needed each other.

Lennie, God doesn't waste a thing. He just doesn't go bumbling around doing things "accidentally." There is a reason and a purpose behind every small incident in our lives, just as surely as the hairs on our head are numbered. (And the way some of us "tease" ours, I'll bet there is a "head" bookkeeper going insane trying to keep our count untangled. Gene says as fast as his are falling out, he hopes they are using computers.)

I am so entirely dependent upon the Lord for the protection of this brood. I find that some mothers measure their love on a "worry-mometer." They prove their love by the amount of worrying they do. This is futile and useless, devil-inspired, and God-grieving. Lennie, once a child is more than an arm's length away, there is nothing you can do to protect him, but to trust a holy, all-seeing, all-knowing God to watch over him. And he has proven Himself over and over again to me.

Besides the incident with Don, a number of years ago, Laurie was struck by a car on U.S. 33, and the words of the officer were—"She was thrown thirty feet—that child should be dead!" She came through with one scar, a black and blue, dirt-entrenched body, and a set of chastened parents, much wiser for the wear.

Do you remember when Don was underneath Mr. Oaks' car, and no one knew it? He was only about four. He was intently picking out the tiny pebbles from the deep treads of Mr. Oaks' brand new car. Mr. Oaks got in the car, never dreaming Don was under it . . . and the car wouldn't start. He tried three times. Nothing. The motor wouldn't even turn over! Then a scream came from Mrs. Oaks as she saw Don under the back tire from her kitchen window. Mr. Oaks leaped from the car, grabbed Don and whacked him firmly in the provided area, then ran in to fan Mrs. Oaks, back out to his new car—that started promptly—while a little boy was screaming at the top of his lungs—from his nice, safe bedroom.

Do you believe in the protective care of the Lord? I sure do. And when these big hulking boys of mine, and these beautiful little girls are facing the strong temptations they are bound to face during the dating years, what do I do? I take them aside when the time is right, and tearfully, I let them know that there was a time when I didn't know the Lord—and my tastes then were hardly for the pure and holy things. I let them know of problems I had because no one ever told me about Jesus.

Then I turn them loose in this great big wicked world that is just waiting to gobble them up, and then I get on my knees and ask this same Heavenly Father to cover them with the same protective care that kept them safe through auto accidents, tornadoes, and tree falls.

Have they always heeded? I'm not sure. But I know this has made for awfully strong communication in this home. True, sometimes they tell too much. They do it to see the reaction—to hurt, to shock, in some cases a part of the rebellion that hasn't quite worked its way out yet.

But I always try to keep this in mind: there is no sin they can commit, nothing they can take, nothing they can drink that compares with the sin of rejecting Jesus Christ and not giving him the rightful place in their lives. This is the gross sin of any human life—Christ-rejection. The asserting of "self."

It is a real concern to me that my two oldest children do not have an all-consuming love for my Lord.

Could it be because all through their childhood years, they saw hypocrisy in me? I told them about a God of love, but He became a legalistic God, a God of "do's and don'ts" who never quite came through to them as Joy. Or Peace. Or maybe even Love, because of a neurotic and unstable mother whose life didn't line up with the Jesus she talked about.

Well, as I said, God doesn't waste a thing. If I didn't believe He were perfectly capable of picking up all these pieces and putting them together *His* way, I couldn't go on!

If I let all the blunders I've made in the past years (plus all the blunders I am bound to make in the future), stand in my way, my witness would be paralyzed!

More later.

Char

LETTER TWELVE

Dear Lennie,

This one is a dilly. Are you ready?

Gene and I just got back from one of those incentive trips they give to deserving salesmen.

We went to Hawaii.

Sounds innocent enough, doesn't it?

But what a trip! By the time we got home, I'd been torn completely apart, and thanks to a wonderful God—all put back together again.

It all started like this.

As we were about to board the plane, someone said, "Wait! Sheri's not here yet! Hold the plane!"

And suddenly, amidst a flurry of wig cases, tinkling bracelets and clicking heels, Sheri appeared on the scene—without her husband.

Like I said—sounds innocent enough, doesn't it?

It didn't take me long to find out we were in for trouble.

Before I could even adjust my seat-belt, Sheri the Innocent became Sheri the Impossible.

The fact that she and my husband made mudpies together years ago seemed to give her some kind of claim to a coy need for protection.

I heard, "Gene, would you . . . ? Gene, I wonder if . . . Gene, you are such a doll, how do I . . ." so many times, I considered changing his name to Sam.

I contented myself half-heartedly with the book I was reading, thinking it would all pass and drawing satisfaction from the fact that my hubbie seemed a bit disgusted with the whole thing.

I'd never had reason to mistrust him, and I hardly felt her onslaughts were enough to cause me concern now.

But what I hadn't counted on was one solid week of this.

I thought the feelings that I felt building up within me were unimportant—that I was just having a teensy bit of a problem with wifely jealousy—that if I told Gene of my feelings, he'd just say I was being silly, and that I should straighten up.

I am not implying that my husband is not understanding—I'm merely trying to make you aware of the subtleties of Satan when he has the upper hand.

Many emotions stirred within me.

Anxieties—feelings of somehow being threatened—uncomfortable, unexplainable feelings—a hurt I didn't even want to confess.

I remember getting even a time or two.

Like the time we were at dinner and because we'd been laughing so much (I'd long ago learned to cover up an aching heart with a bit of hilarity) my mascara had begun to run.

I said, "I really shouldn't even bother with this stuff. Everytime I put it on my three eye-lashes, I look like Minnie Mouse."

A gale of laughter.

Sheri said, "But darling—I think if *I* only had three eye-lashes I'd wear *false* ones!"

So I remarked a bit caustically, "But darling—anyone who'd wear false eye-lashes—would wear false *anything!*"

It meant getting tomato juice cleaned off Gene's tie, but it was worth every penny.

On the beach, it was the same.

Me and my inferiorities had taken a deep breath and hoped people would think of me as the fruit tree that was gnarled and bent from bearing so much fruit (people always said "Hey—you look great—for having had six kids!") so me and my inferiorities sidled in and out of the bikinis almost as though we belonged.

Shari's project for the day was to get her picture taken with her arms around Gene because she had this pastor, who—of all things—wanted her to get "freed up."

I muttered to myself—"If she gets any *more* freed up, she'll get arrested for soliciting!"

On and on it went. Gene ducked away from

71

her at every opportunity. Although I drew much consolation from this, my feelings were more than I could handle.

Things kept getting worse and worse for me. I am ashamed to admit this, but I didn't even know this was an out and out Satanic attack until we were on our way home.

I was more than happy to wave a rather disinterested good-bye to the shimmering goddess as she boarded another plane.

By now my dilemma had gotten the best of me.

I was really in a bad way, and began to sob as we came into the house. It was dawn, and I knew Gene was exhausted—but I needed desperately for him to minister to me.

As I confessed having given Satan a good firm foothold, Gene became the priest in our home and held me tenderly and commanded the spirit of jealousy to leave in the Name of Jesus!

We were both awe-struck as this foul spirit wrenched itself from me with sounds I would never have made had the choice been mine! I became freed in that instant, because of the power that is ours in the Name of Jesus.

I became free to see Sheri in a new light. Not as Sheri the Impossible, but Sheri the Desperate—crying out for help. I became free to pray for her, to ask God to step into her life and fill it full of goodness—to meet her heart's needs as only the love of God can do—free to ask Him to deliver her from herself and her conflicts, as He had set me free.

This was our first confrontation with the reality of evil spirits and the magnitude of deliverance. Our hearts were so blessed to know factually that Jesus is sufficient for our every need.

It's just like I said, Lennie—there is no room for boredom in the Spirit-baptized walk. To quote my Gene, "It gets more exciting every day." We don't believe for one moment that God ever intended for His children to be bored with their relationship with Him or with one another, *or* during services.

Isn't it just great to know He is so very much alive?

Well, I must go get the "brood" busy. Sometimes they need a little push.

The other day someone said, "That Laurie is such a doll—what makes her so out-going?"

Jan, who was busy doing Laurie's job at the moment said a bit sarcastically, "I think it's the fact that she hates to be 'in-*doing*.' "

You wouldn't believe those two. Scrapping one moment, and laughing together the next.

You should see Laurie. She is in the first throes of that agonizing stage called "cheer-leading syndrome." She doesn't walk anymore. She bounds. She comes leaping into the room like a gazelle, arms akimbo, or clapping them over her head breathlessly asking, "Mu-thur, Mu-thur, when-do-we-eat! Beardsley! Beardsley! can't-be-BEAT!"

So I leap and jump right behind her—much like a kangaroo—and shout "Laurie-Laurie-set-the-table-on-the-double!   Or-you'll-be-in-for-a-pack-of-trouble!"

Jan just shakes her head and thinks how nice it will be to be married so she can change *her* name.

More later.

Char

LETTER THIRTEEN

Dear Lennie,

Just taking a few minutes to recover from my morning 8:05 trauma, better known as the "where-is-my-book-who-has-my-gloves-I-can't-find-my-other-shoe-he-hit-me-Mom-tie-this-bow" syndrome.

I just put a gooey thing together for the P.T.A. wingding tonight. Laurie walked by, glanced at the recipe and said, "Mom? The recipe says, 'let stand overnight'—shouldn't you have made it last night?"

I said, "Honey, it's dark in the refrigerator. I'll keep the door shut, and it will never know the difference."

There's nothing like a well-organized child when it comes to zeroing in on weaknesses like procrastination!

Speaking of weaknesses, let me share another one the Holy Spirit has been zeroing in on, right down there—just to the left in your rib cage where forgiving takes place—or wherever you keep your "forgiver."

It all started like this.

The other day I overheard someone say, "After all, the Lord expects us to forgive and forget, just the way He does." (Bear in mind we are not talking about "forgetting" in the human sense as opposed to remembering, because it was pointed out to us once that "forgetting" is a human weakness—a loss of memory—but God has said He will "remember our iniquities no more," meaning they are *blotted out!* We have almost weakened our human conception of God's ability to "blot out" our sins, because we have put it into the proverbial cliche "forgive and forget" almost implying that they *could* be remembered again if forgotten!)

Still, the remark kept burning itself into my interior. And immediately, the Minister of my interior got to work on it. As the Holy Spirit and I mulled the thought over in my "mulling over place," some definite ideas began to take shape. Ideas that made me blush just a bit.

You see, for about three weeks I'd been experiencing a lot of personal hurt. I began to think my heart must surely be shaped like a dart board! As the hurts kept coming, I kept forgiving, but I can't say that I did a lot of forgetting.

On several occasions, I found myself going to someone and saying, "Well, so-and-so didn't mean it, and of *course* I've forgiven them, BUT—you'll never believe what they said to me. . . ." And out would come my tale of woe.

I remember repeating a particular "barbed" hurt

to the pastor and piously commenting, "Pastor, I'm *so* ashamed, I shouldn't have repeated that. Now if I were a really mature Christian, I wouldn't have!" as I smugly draped my immaturity more noticeably around me.

Suddenly, I began to see a bit more clearly.

Forgiving is only HALF the battle. Forgetting is the *other* half. Now, "forgetting"—humanly speaking—is the opposite of "memorizing." So, if the way we memorize something is by repeating it OVER AND OVER AGAIN—then it stands to reason that the one way we can forget is by NOT repeating it!

Wow! I couldn't even blame my unwillingness to forget on "lack of maturity" anymore! Maturity had nothing to do with it! Just a plain, basic spiritual truth busily at work doing its own "thing."

Well, it sure adds a new dimension to forgiving, doesn't it?

Love,
Char

LETTER FOURTEEN

Dear Lennie,

Will I ever adjust to teenagers?

Along with pretty teenage girls you get shy thirteen year old boys that are too bashful to tell Laurie she is cute, so they relay the message by draping our front yard trees with toilet paper! (And it's only April! Those poor little buds think they have been wrapped in swaddling clothes!)

I find gawky young lads leaning against doorways, car fenders, fence rails—straddled over bikes, porch banisters, and kitchen stools.

When we made a firm rule that none of these species are ever to be found draped or leaning anywhere on the premises unless an adult is present, I heard the proverbial cry, "But mother! Don't you trust me?" I wondered how many times that one little phrase has reverberated down through the ages!

"Honey—to be real honest—I don't. But before you take it too personally, go get your Bible—there's something in it you need to read, underline, memorize, absorb and clip to your innermost

78

being. Turn to Jeremiah 17—and I think you'll find it about verse 9."

We were baking cookies together at the time. She set the timer, then went for her Bible and obediently read, "The heart is deceitful above all things, and desperately wicked: who can know it?" I was grateful for her submission. I'm not so sure I wouldn't have clenched my teeth a time or two at having scriptural principles tossed at me for every situation.

"Now, sweetheart—I'd like to go on record as saying I didn't write that—God did—through His servant Jeremiah. Now, if God says your heart is deceitful and wicked surely you can believe it. What's more—my heart is JUST as deceitful and wicked—because that Book was written for me as well as for you. What I'm trying to say is—you should learn early in life that you can't trust yourself—or any boy! Because *all* hearts are deceitful and wicked. The old nature that we like to think of as dead can be just as readily revived to life as the new nature God has put in us."

She seemed really thoughtful. I was so grateful I could rely upon the Word of God for having the right answers. I sure would hate to have to handle situations like this with just mere human wisdom.

"Now—as is so often the case, there is another side of the coin. Though our hearts are deceitful and desperately wicked, we can be obedient to the Word of God and the Spirit of God within us, and pretty much stay out of trouble."

I began to draw a little diagram in the flour on the counter top. The diagram consisted of several little arches one on top of the other.

"According to the Word of God, we are in a place of safety if we are right with God and rightly related to one another. Down here under this bottom arch is your place of safety. See? 'Children obey your parents.' The requirements are not too stiff. You just have to trust our judgment: we've learned most of our lessons through hard knocks before we came to the Lord. Then, you *obey* our instructions—thereby staying under the covering of safety God has provided for you. The next arch up is mine. As long as I submit to Daddy, I'm in the place of protection God has provided for me. One bit of veering to the right or left of that protective covering and I become a prime target for Satan— because veering to either side would be coming out from under submission—and steering straight towards rebellion with both eyes open! Under this arch is safety for me. The next arch belongs to Daddy. He is under Christ—who is under God, although equal to Him in office. And under Him in submission by choice."

She took a sheet of cookies out. While she was removing them, I went on.

"Honey, there are so many promises of protection in the Word of God. But only if we meet the conditions. If we've veered in any direction from under our "covering" of safety we can expect trouble—because out there in the area of rebellion is where Satan is his busiest, and he has the right of way."

I'd made a big exclamation point out of chocolate chips alongside of the diagram for emphasis. But by this time the odor had wafted into the family room, and hordes of little ones from various parts of the house and neighborhood poured hungrily into the kitchen with eager sniffing.

I'd been so glad for our chat. And this way of teaching Biblical principles has been so much more rewarding than "thou shalt nots."

Now all I had to do was determine how many cookies *I* dared to eat before I left the safety of discipline and stepped into the area of sinning.

More later—

Char

LETTER FIFTEEN

Dear Lennie!

How shall I start?

How can you squeeze joy, wonder, awe, heartache, pathos, and the miraculous into intelligible sentences? How do you bottle up a flood-tide of emotion into a paragraph?

How do you measure a miracle?

I can only try.

It all started out with a phone call on one of those crisp October days that lets you know you needn't panic anymore if you forgot to bring the milk in, and that soon the kids'll be scrapping over who has to wear the mitten with the hole in it.

The phone call was from Beth's mother.

I think the fact that Beth is my niece is insignificant because the tie that binds our hearts is spiritual, not physical. You wouldn't remember her anyhow as she was probably selling Girl Scout cookies while you and I were swapping recipes.

But the fact that Beth lived in Key Biscayne, Florida, at the time of this story *is* significant because it proves that distance and seemingly impossible circumstances mean nothing to the Lord.

As I talked with Hazel (her mother) I detected a distinguishable tremor in her voice that lets even a slightly discerning woman know a heartache is being smothered beneath a lot of unnecessary trivia.

I waited for the thin veneer of the conversation to crack so I could get a glimpse underneath of the real reason for her call.

It didn't take too long.

I finally said, "Hazel, what's wrong?"

She burst into tears. "It's Beth—she's going to divorce Bert, and I can hardly bear to think of little Sean suffering that—after—after . . ."

She was no longer coherent. I told her I'd be over shortly and that, yes, I felt sure the Lord could heal a marriage again if He'd done it for Gwen and Ted, and yes, He'd straightened us out —of course He could do it again.

But the Charlene that fell to her knees after hanging up the phone was a little less confident than the Charlene on the phone.

I cried out to the Lord in anguish because I was becoming more and more aware of Satan's attacks against the homelife of America. And now my darling niece was being led astray by this great Deceiver.

I prayed in the Spirit most of the time. Then I prayed, "Lord, You *did* do it for us, and for Gwen and Ted—surely You can do the same for Beth and Bert. Lord, they've been through so much. Please send us to them, Lord!"

Immediately the Enemy screamed into my ear, "Do you think you are His *only* answer to marriage problems? You're asking too much. It's impossible."

And then I remembered that after all, they *were* in Florida, and I was praying in a riot of Hoosier autumn color 1500 miles away from them. It did seem like I was asking a lot.

And so, being very green in this business of miracles and pointed petitions, I gave in to Satan's taunts and changed my prayer to, "If that's asking too much, Lord, then get someone to them who knows You well enough to handle the situation." And I cried my heart out for some long time, because I loved these two worldings deeply.

As I prayed, I kept seeing Beth before me—Beth in a little ballet tu-tu, tip-toeing her way into everyone's heart—Beth, the beautiful, sailing off to college so full of hope—Beth, the sophisticate, married to a wonderful guy named Bert, both being disillusioned about the "exciting life" of social climbing and cocktail parties.

. . . And then . . . and then I saw Beth again. Beth, the unconsolable, being held by neighbors as the thin wail of the siren approached to pick up the lifeless body of little Scotty, one of her two-year-old twins from the driveway.

I saw the neighbor that couldn't be comforted. Poor fellow. He'd only wanted to use Beth's driveway to unload stone in that corner of his back yard. Tragedy struck when he offered to move Beth's car out.

It was done, and couldn't be undone. Who could say why it happened? Who knows? Only God.

And now . . . divorce.

I couldn't accept it.

Bert himself had come from a broken home and still carried scars from this wound. I knew he needed a home life he could rely on. His hope had been that he and Beth would never go this route. I knew they had loved each other very much at one time, and I firmly believed that any two people who see enough in one another to attract them to the altar can have that same love revived again by the breath of the Holy Spirit, and I refused to believe any other way. And I refused to think anything but positively about the whole situation.

And so, I took the request before the fellowship, and many were praying with us.

One sub-zero day in January (so sub-zero that I had to panic all over again if I *did* forget to bring the milk in), Gene announced while sweeping the snow off his feet that "the trip we won . . . the one we gave to Phil (our store manager) . . . looks like we will have to take it. Phil says he doesn't feel well . . . you only have a week . . . can you get ready?"

I'm sure you will think I'm absolutely insane for even having to give it a second thought, but even trips can be a chore when they are so close together, and we'd just been on one. But this one was a Caribbean cruise . . . and when I glanced

85

at the three bottles of frozen milk he'd just brought in, somehow I thought I could get ready.

So I said, "Well—if we *have* to.—Does this one start in New York like the other cruise did?"

Calmly, he said, "No, Miami."

I catapulted out of the chair and into his arms and shrieked, "Gene! The Lord is in it! Don't you see? Miami is only a stone's throw from Key Biscayne! Good heavens—poor Phil—I don't understand it! Most people would go on a Caribbean cruise if they had to go in an *iron lung!* But this is God's way of answering our prayers! Oh, He is *so* wonderful!" And I kept smothering him with kisses, and managed to maim him with my wire rims, like I always do.

As he nursed the one eye I'd poked, he said, "Hold on, Joan-of-Arc! We'd only have a few hours with them at the boat dock! You can hardly hold a revival there—and, as I recall, they weren't exactly Sunday School material."

But I kept smothering him with kisses and shouting "Hallelujahs" and refusing to listen to any negative thoughts he might be entertaining, because I was convinced God was in it!

There had been times when I wanted to wheedle a bit and say, "Gene, couldn't we just drive down to Florida?" but I knew if I did that, I couldn't be sure of God's timing. I knew *He* had to get us there, and I never dreamed it would be this way!

Lennie, it is so great to watch Him work—to feel His presence—and to be assured of His presence even when we *can't* feel it. This is truly living abundantly!

But it's time for supper and you-know-who forgot to take anything out of the deep-freeze, so I've got to devise something tasty—and fast.

I've often wondered why they couldn't insert a personal, "Ladies, did you remember to take something out of the deep-freeze for dinner?" with every morning newscast like they put in those in-the-interest-of-the-public things.

More later—
Love,
Char

LETTER SIXTEEN

Dear Lennie,

I'm suffering from an acute attack of "author-itis." A rainy day like today always brings it on. The only remedy is to get the kids busy with train tracks and cookie baking and "make straight paths for my feet" toward the typewriter. The stereo stacatto of the rain and my beloved typewriter make the malady quite enjoyable—especially when I smell the coffee and the fresh-baked pineapple cookies.

But "author-itis" it is! And so, until something is published, I can only refer to my malady as "an interesting hobby—really great therapy," which makes people scratch their heads and repress snickers. But I put on my most tolerant look, for I'm well aware that "a prophet is honored every-where, *except* in his own country, and among his *own* people" (TLB Matthew 13:57; italics mine). Then I pray earnestly that my "look" came through as tolerant, and not, "Oh, just you wait and see!"

Anyway, the thoughts keep rolling in, and it will all make the wildest diary for my grandchildren to pore over! But when they pore over it, I don't want them to think, "I wonder who that Lennie was. . . ." I want them to exclaim, "Oh, I must have Grandma's Jesus for my own!"

Anyway let me get back to my story before your curiosity wanes.

Just before we went on our trip to the Caribbean, the fellowship gave us a sendoff I'll never forget. Truly, you'd have thought we *were* going off to the Crusades.

I'd phoned Beth to let her know the approximate hours we'd be at the boat dock, and she'd said rather nervously, "Char, Bert doesn't know that any of you up North know of our problem—please don't mention it, will you?"

Well, that didn't seem like much of an opener, but I was trusting the Lord to do this thing His way, not mine.

So-o-o, we went off on our cruise, which was a most lovely one. We had ample time to dig into the Word, to spend time with Him and prepare our hearts for whatever the Lord had in mind.

And so the cruise came to an end. The weather was so fantastic in Miami—and so rotten in Indiana, we made the daring decision to stay a few days—which was quite a sacrifice since the return flight was charter. But like I said, God was in it. Even to the rotten weather in Indiana.

Beth came to meet us. How my heart ached when she came through those gates. She'd lost the little-girl softness I'd remembered. I thought tragedy would serve to soften and mellow her, but instead I saw a flirtatious little blonde bombshell, busily trying to smother all the seething resentments and hurts she was carrying inside. And Bert —dear Bert. The loss of Scotty had almost undone him. And now, the added burden of divorce.

He'd been going to a psychiatrist because of his emotional problems, and whatever problems the psychiatrist couldn't handle, he took to the dark lounge near his office.

The estrangement was so thick between them, I could have scooped it up with a soup ladle. I whispered, "Lord, have we bitten off more than we can chew?"

I watched Beth as she flitted restlessly about. She seemed a bit uncomfortable and reluctant to let the conversation get away from her in any direction she couldn't control. Bert was unusually quiet.

They'd picked us up on a Saturday morning. We spent most of our time getting "re-acquainted" as we hadn't seen each other for over a year since Scotty's funeral.

Interestingly enough, God had confirmed our being there in a most beautiful way. Beth and I were alone on Saturday afternoon. As we talked, I touched on a few significant things. I happened to have Pat Boone's book, *A New Song,* which I'd brought for her—said I thought she'd enjoy it. Then I asked her if she had read the recent article in the *Look* magazine about the Jesus movement

—hoping to be able to share our experience with her, using that as a stepping stone. (You know, some of that good 'ole manipulation business of the past—as though the Holy Spirit couldn't handle things all by Himself.)

Well, it didn't open any doors. But we did talk for quite awhile about her load of grief, and how bad things were between Bert and her. They'd lost all communication with one another, and things were so bad between them that they moved flat against the wall when passing in their narrow corridor so they wouldn't have to risk touching one another. She told me the divorce papers were on her lawyer's desk waiting to be signed, but she had put it off until Monday because she didn't want to ruin our few hours together. She also admitted being reluctant about signing them. But the doctor had told her she should. (Good 'ole Doc.)

He said, "Once you have emotional problems, you *always* have emotional problems."

In the meantime, Bert was wondering what in the world you do with people who are religious, other than go to church? So valiantly he said to Gene, "We have a real fine preacher here on the island—er, uh—he's Presbyterian. I've heard him once or twice. He's really interesting. . . ."

I couldn't help feeling a bit sorry for him. He wanted so much to please us, and to do what we would enjoy. We were not sure that a Presbyterian would have much to offer us, but we said, "That's a great idea. We'd love to go."

And so, on Sunday morning, we went off a bit reluctantly to a Presbyterian church where we were all prepared to be bored to death.

The place was so packed, we couldn't even sit together.

And within just a few minutes, we knew why it was so packed. Here was a man of God who wasn't afraid to speak the Word of God! And not only did he come forth with a real message that could stir the heart, but he talked of exactly the three things Beth and I had discussed on the afternoon before.

He said, "Did any of you see the article in *Look* magazine? Don't be too condemning, and keep your eye on this movement, for I believe it is of God."

Then the rest of his message was about human suffering—how it can make you bitter, or it can strengthen you to receive from God, and to help you on to maturity.

Then halfway through his message, he said, "By the way, I couldn't go to sleep last night until I'd finished the Pat Boone book. There are some things in it that are controversial, such as the baptism of the Holy Spirit, and speaking in tongues . . . but no one can deny that Pat has had a tremendous experience with God. . . ." And then this vibrant young man went on with his message.

Beth marveled at this. She really didn't know what to think! She said (aside to me after the service), "It's uncanny! It's as though he were in the room with us yesterday!

I whispered, "Honey, you haven't seen *any*thing yet!"

Our afternoon was pleasant. We toured the island and glimpsed the trees behind which stood the "Florida White House," and watched the helicopters take off, wondering what important people might be in them as they loomed up from the President's "copter pad."

That evening, after a scrumptious meal Beth prepared for us, we sat around her dining room table talking about everything—everything but the Truth. My heart ached. Here were two kids who desperately needed the Truth, and we had the Truth, the Way *and* the Life—but getting it from our lives into theirs *had* to be the work of the Holy Spirit, and so we just waited . . . waiting for Him to open a door. We'd been walking "this way" long enough to know that when He opens the door, there are no creaking hinges . . . only an awareness . . . a discerning of the anointed "now."

So we waited.

And then, ever so gently Jesus said, "Now."

He gave us the opening we'd been waiting for, when Beth asked about Gwen, whom she had known only slightly. We began to tell them how the Lord had moved upon their hearts, and about their problems (realizing they were similar to Beth and Bert's).

And then, in hushed tones we told them of our own problems. We told them of the deafening silence that can grow out of a communication gap when a marriage begins to lose vitality.

Oh, Lennie, read reverently. The re-opening of old wounds was painful for us. Indeed, we couldn't have done it if a Tender Physician hadn't been present with us to make it easy.

We went through all the things I've already related to you. Lennie, you'll never know what it meant to me—to see Gene sharing these things with them—when only a few months before he would not have been willing to share, or even to admit that we had a problem. The tears on his face shimmered in the light of the candle, and touched a chord in Bert's heart.

Bert said, "But what about Scotty? Why would a God of love allow a thing like that?"

His eyes followed Beth as she went to tuck little Sean into bed. I sensed only a touch of the heartache they must have been experiencing as every glance at Sean was a constant reminder that once there were two—exactly alike—but now there was only one doing all the antics and asking the childish questions that little Scotty would be doing and asking—if Scotty were here.

Even the velvet glow of the candle couldn't erase the grimness on Bert's face as he remembered—

the car rolling out of the driveway—a quick cry. A thud. Gripping terror. The lifeless form. He'd relived it a thousand times in nightmares already.

I got out my Bible and read quietly the account in II Samuel, chapter 12. He quickly identified with King David and the loss of the child born to him and Bathsheba. The words, "can I bring him back again? I shall go to him—but he shall not return unto me" seemed to burn deep into his heart.

Beth had slipped back into her chair. As I glanced at her, I felt a sense of wonder. Could it be?

Yes, it was true. The little-girl softness had returned. I was certain He was at it again—that He was doing a mighty work within their hearts in His own inimitable fashion! I could see that the grimness was gone from Bert's face too.

We took their hands and prayed. Love enveloped us . . . embraced and pervaded us . . . Tangible Love . . . Love Eternal. We in Him . . . and He in us.

The next morning I heard Beth humming softly as she prepared breakfast.

"Here, Auntie, . . ." as she thrust something into my hands. "When we have guests it's customary for someone to pick the dry cereal out of the sugar bowl, and you are the chosen one!" She let out a little giggle as she went back to cutting the grapefruit.

Bert came swinging through the kitchen and

pecked us on the cheek while adjusting his tie. He had to hurry off to work. I hated to see him go—we'd be leaving that morning, and I knew it would be quite some time before we'd see him again.

But when he'd driven out of sight, Beth began to tell us—yes, through tears . . . tears that were fresh with bright hope for the future . . . tears of happiness and deep longing.

"Oh, Char . . . Gene . . . for the first time in almost two years he took me into his arms and said, 'Beth, I love you! With God's help we can make it, Beth! I know we can!' "

Excitedly, she went on. Some sentences coherent, some not—but no one really cared.

She cried, "He told me that the trips to the psychiatrist wouldn't be necessary anymore—or the trips to the lounge. He said something happened inside of him last night—that the load of grief over Scotty just seemed to lift as we prayed. And, Char! All the hostilities I had for Bert—they're gone! They're absolutely *gone*!"

Her face was radiant. My face was wet. So was Gene's. A God of Love had made another marriage whole.

And I know you are probably thinking this is the end of the story. Well, go blow your nose, and I'll tell you the rest. Because, like so many of the things the Lord does, this was only the beginning.

We'd dropped Beth off at her office. She looked like a new bride. I wondered if she'd ever be able to concentrate on her work! I didn't call her for two days. We made our way North and stopped here and there to visit relatives. But Beth and Bert were not out of our thoughts for a moment.

I knew they had so many questions—so many things they wanted to know. One of their questions had been "but where will we find any prayer meetings like yours down here in Florida?" Gene and I assured them that God would lead them to the meetings. During the course of our talk that Beth and I had had on Saturday, she'd told me about a new friend, a lady named Ann, who had been the compassionate "listener" Beth had so sorely needed through this heartbreak.

When I called Beth, she said breathlessly, "Char, I thought you'd never call! I have so much to tell you! We are so happy—happier than we've ever been in our lives—and Ann—remember her? She called me about a half-hour after you left—remember how I told you she kept telling me I needed a miracle? Well, I told her I'd had my miracle—and did she know anything about any charismatic meetings in the area? She just laughed and said, 'Beth, honey, I thought you'd never ask! I've been going to meetings for three months, and just didn't want to push it on you!' "

Lennie, can you see why we get so excited?

Well, Beth and Bert *did* go to the meetings and both went on to receive the baptism of the Holy Spirit. And when the Lord zapped them, He really zapped them! These kids have gone on to turn practically the whole island upside down!

Every Monday night you can see a stream of the most incongruous combinations wending their way to Beth and Bert's house. Hippies, kids half-stoned, divorcées, the immoral—all making their way to hear about a God of Love Who cares—to hear Bert tell them, "There is nothing you can do to cause God to love you more—there is nothing you can do to cause God to love you less. His love is constant, sure and unmoveable."

I am happy to tell you that as I type this, Beth is expecting again—and it looks as though it could be another multiple birth! Isn't Jesus wonderful?

Love,
Char

LETTER SEVENTEEN

Dear Lennie,

Praise God for all the good things He is doing on the inside! Listen to this: today is one of those drizzly slate-gray days—and I didn't even know it—until someone told me!

Now that's progress, because two years ago my disposition would have been entirely dependent upon the weatherman's prediction!

But now I've learned that I can be just as enthusiastically happy on these gray days as I can on golden yellow ones. I mean, after all, why not? The only difference is their color!

Jesus is the same yesterday, today, and forever—and our disposition should be shaping up likewise.

Must tell you what happened over the weekend. My Gene was like a bear. And I don't mean "cuddly" bear. You know the old story. Too much work, too many hours, not enough help, too many pressures, etc.

Well, something happened to cause me to "hurt." Now you have no idea how much I'd love to tell you all about the hurt in minute detail, but the Lord is causing me to "prove all things" I've been preaching to others—like not repeating hurts because it makes a deeper impression in your memory, and such—well, I'm afraid that even includes spilling it all over a letter that will never get mailed, because I'm discovering how much our demanding "self-lives" that we think are so dead get great satisfaction from sharing these hurts with others.

(Think for a moment. When someone says, "Oh, you poor thing!" we snivel and dab at those little unholy tears, and draw our solace from the arm of flesh, instead of the heart of God.)

Well, anyhow—I thought, "I'll give the dear an opportunity to apologize, even though he doesn't deserve it!" to which he didn't respond at all.

So there I was:

Face to face with a resentment that wouldn't quit. Everytime I rolled it over on the Lord, it came rolling right back, "bigger and better." I heaved, I pushed. Nothing. It was there and I was stuck with it.

I went dutifully about my business, which happened to be slamming things around the kitchen, at the time. (Ever notice how rebellion shows up this way?)

Well, while slamming, I heard a Voice say quietly, and yet with thunderous authority, "Let a wife see that she reverence her husband." No more. No less. He didn't say, "Let a wife see that she reverence her husband only when he is loving her as Christ loved the Church." And He didn't say, "Let a wife see that she reverence her husband when she feels up to it." And He didn't say, "Let a wife see that she reverence her husband when others are around."

He didn't say, "I'll drape reverence around you." He said, "Let the wife SEE that she reverence her husband." He'd put the responsibility squarely upon my shoulders.

Immediately I ran for my Amplified Bible to look into this. And when I read the full meaning of what "reverence" means, I seemed to hear an amplified, "NOW HEAR THIS!" For the Amplified Bible wrings the full meaning out of this little, neglected word.

To "reverence" means the wife ". . . notices him (husband), regards him, honors him . . . praises him, and loves and admires him exceedingly" (Ephesians 5:33).

Also in I Peter 3:2 we read, "adore him (husband) in the human sense, be devoted to, deeply love and enjoy your husband." Wow! What's in a word!

And in Ephesians 5:22 it says we should do all this as "unto the Lord." It all began to settle in on me. To honor, love and praise our husbands was to honor and praise the Lord! Could you imagine scolding Jesus because he was late for dinner? Did all this mean that to be short-tempered and impatient with our husbands meant being impatient and short-tempered with our very own Creator?

It was the lever I needed to roll that nasty resentment over where it belonged! (Finally! I sure was glad to be rid of it!) This bit of scripture swept through my whole being and flushed the resentment clean away, and I was "free" again.

Well, Lennie—must go now. Because the king is coming! And he's coming home for dinner, so I'd better "get with it."

More later,
Char

LETTER EIGHTEEN

Dear Lennie,

Gene had to be "out on the road" again this week.

When he came in on Friday, I said, "Who goes there? Friend or foe?"

He scooped me into his arms and said, "Your husband, you kook!" And I knew he wasn't going to be a bear. He acknowledged he'd been "bearish" the weekend before, but that the Lord had taken care of it all. Interestingly enough, I had determined I was going to "reverence-him-no-matter-what," but he has been such a doll, it has been no chore.

He is indeed loving me "as Christ loved the Church," and I don't know much about this "without spot and wrinkle" business, because I have a cold sore and magnified crow's feet peeking from behind my wire-rims—but I guess that doesn't apply to the physical anyhow, does it?

How I praise the Lord for such a loving husband —and how I praise the Lord for the "rough spots," because He wastes nothing—there is a lesson to be gained in every experience!

Guess what. Jamie wanted some tympany sticks. Now I didn't feel any particular leading to go out and buy tympany sticks for a six year old with a drummer complex, but I *did* do something constructive.

(I usually don't give in to him so easily, but he loves music so much—and tymp sticks would be *so* much quieter) so I stuck fresh marshmallows on two unsharpened pencils, wrapped them in a plastic wrap, tied them neatly with thread and trimmed off the excess, and we came up with a pair of the neatest tymp sticks in town! I have to make fresh ones every day, but it doesn't take long. It sure shakes company up, though, if he marches in and announces, "Mom, I just ate my tympany sticks—could you make me some more?"

I am so grateful for an understanding Father who knew that mothers would need bits of ingenuity along the way to get the job done! (I still can't balance a checkbook, though.)

Love,
Char

LETTER NINETEEN

Dear Lennie,

Well, the "king" will soon be coming home to his royal palace. He's been gone for two weeks and it seems like an eternity! Yet, more and more the Lord is teaching me how to have abundant life with—or without—the presence of my husband.

I can honestly say it's been a difficult lesson to learn.

And if I were to be even more honest, I guess I'd share with you an out-and-out rebellious streak I experienced this summer.

You see, Gene has started a second business. Don is managing the store quite nicely now, and Gene has always wanted to diversify, so he started a business he's always wanted to try his hand at. Only one thing—it takes him away from home even more than the first one did!

Well, this summer it really "got to me." I began to resent his having to be gone so much. One night, I threw a tantrum bigger and better than Shakespeare's shrew ever thought of throwing. I pounded the pillow—I cried, pouted and was just generally obnoxious. I asserted a whole pocketful of ugly self-will and shouted, "I won't live like this! I won't stand for another business to come between us! I refuse to submit to it!" And because pillow pounding felt so good, I did some more of it.

My, what a wise husband I have. There was no retaliation. He didn't even chide me for acting so little like a Christian. He just waited for the storm to subside and said, "For right now—this seems to be the will of God for my life."

He knew that any moment the Holy Spirit would begin to minister to me. And He did. I slowly began to speak out the things the Lord was saying to me deep down inside of me. I stopped my snubbing long enough to say, "Then, I'm rebelling against the Lord?"

I, who had so often told young women with problems that "your circumstances are determined through the one over you in authority," was not practicing what I had been preaching!

I realized that my nasty reaction to these circumstances was out and out rebellion against God.

You see, I wanted a "four o'clock" husband. I've always wanted that, I guess. He would come in, play with the kids, we'd eat a well-balanced meal promptly at five, then we'd do family things together, then we'd all march off to bed and start all over again the next day. My flesh cried out for this kind of existence.

But then the Word of God comes into my life.

It puts something in my way. It reveals to me the fact that a wife should submit to her own husband —that she should "adapt" to him (that's in Phillip's translation). Not *he* to *me*—or *my* desires—or *my* whims. The Word of God also imposed another restraint to this desire. It said I should "learn" to be content. It didn't say that contentment was going to be draped over me. It involved "learning" —and learning always involves "lessons."

As I lay there snubbing and rebelling, I couldn't help thinking of the shape the household was in. I'd been grouchy as a bear to the kids—because all I could concentrate on was getting my own way. I was joyless, unenthusiastic. The Lord hadn't brought anyone my way to be ministered to for quite some time. All of a sudden, I realized I was "on the shelf." I saw that because of my rebellion, no one was being drawn any closer to the Lord. Because of my rebellion, joy was gone. Suddenly, I was very sick of my own selfish "self" and very ready to repent.

So I cried all the harder, but this time the tears were the tears of a penitent. I asked my husband's forgiveness for having caused him so much hurt. I asked the Lord's forgiveness for rebelling so against the circumstances He'd set me in. I asked the kids' forgiveness for being so grouchy—told them I'd been temporarily derailed, but hoped to be going full steam again soon. My joy returned, and with it a deeper determination to submit wholly, as in the sight of God.

Then I began the arduous task of "setting the shewbread" in order. I was determined that I would line my will up directly in line with the will of God. (In Exodus, the shewbread depicts the will of man. These little loaves were to be lined up precisely in order—six in one line, six in line just beneath.) I was tired of my will being all heaped up together. The loaves of my "shewbread" looked like a day-old bake sale!

I determined to clean up on murmuring and complaining. It had to cease. In its place I would put gratefulness for anything I was tempted to murmur and complain about. It's a real spiritual exercise, but it strengthens like a muscle and the more you do it the easier it becomes.

By developing a grateful heart, I found a more submissive attitude beginning to take over. You can talk about submission until you are blue in the face, but if it doesn't become a heart attitude, it will be nothing but head knowledge.

The refusal to murmur and complain meant accepting whatever God should bring into my life, calmly. Even if the milk got spilled, my best china got broken, my husband was late for dinner, or my friend's children tore up my furniture. I found I could determine my attachment to "things" by my reaction to their removal or their destruction.

Then I discovered this determination had a lot to do with killing out self-love. For it's self-love that screams out over the spilled milk, because it didn't want to be bothered. It's self-love that complains when a husband is late for dinner because YOU wanted his presence. It's self-love that hurts when china is broken, because it has such a hold on you because of its price and beauty. And if you think I'm looney, just remember that "where your treasure is, there will your heart be also."

Well, since the king is coming, guess I'd better get his royal palace in shape. I'll have to check the refrigerator and make sure there aren't more than three empty catsup bottles, and ditch the little cups of moldy peas. (But it's SO much easier to throw them out when they are moldy.) Must turn out all basement, attic, and closet lights—that have probably been on all the time he's been gone. I had the car washed, and the oil checked—and all the McDonald's wrappers removed. Oh, the checkbook. Must get it balanced. He doesn't see a thing romantic about those little love notes when I'm overdrawn that say "P.S. I love you," in the deposit column.

Love,
Char

LETTER TWENTY

Dear Lennie,

Satan found a chink in my armor, and a persistent flu-bug made its way into my interior. (I'm convinced that if God is the Giver of everything that is good, then flu-bugs don't come from Him. If illness is from the hand of Satan then it can be rebuked, refused and resisted! And when I get real spiritual, I'll let you know what I did wrong.)

But praise the Lord, it didn't stop God's timetable even one little bit! Here's what happened.

I was sitting here typing, and feebly rebuking while all bundled up in an afghan to combat the chills, when the telephone rang. It was Gene's cousin, Vicki. I could see she was just as bubbly over the phone as she was in a room full of people. But in just a few seconds I could tell it was the old familiar cover-up. The gaiety, the clowning—but the underneath "something" clamoring "help me—help me."

She laughed her happy laugh and said; "Whatcha' doin'?"

"Honey, if I told you—you'd never believe me."

"Try me."

"I'm writing a book—"

"You're *kidding!*" and, as usual, the gale of laughter that always accompanies the disbelief that a kookie housewife could possibly have anything to say that the rest of the world would want to hear.

Once she got control of herself, she said ". . . about what?"

"Well, about me—and Gene—and Jesus." (And about here I thought, "Now why did I say that? This little worldling could care less!")

But she became very serious. "Char, that's why I'm calling. I've really been going through something, and I can't find anyone to help me. Your name has been going through my mind, and I heard you were some kind of "fanatic" nut. Can I talk to you somewhere where it's quiet?"

My heart sank. I felt so sick and feverish. I didn't know *what* to do. I told her I was not feeling well, but would be happy to talk with her in a couple of days. I hung the phone up and went back to typing, chilling, and rebuking. About a half-hour later, the phone rang again.

It was Vicki. "Char, I know you don't feel well —but I can't wait another minute. I've got to get right with the Lord RIGHT NOW! Can I please come over?" (By now it was almost nine o'clock.)

I took a glance at the house that had a touch more than just a lived-in-look. I knew the fever was raging within me. Kids weren't bedded down yet. But I said "Of course. Give me about one half hour. Come on over."

As I was getting the kids ready for bed, I couldn't help thinking that this had to be a miracle. Vicki just wasn't the "type" that would blurt something out like that unless she was really serious—which she wasn't, usually—about anything. Because our "interests" were not the same, we hadn't gotten to know each other very well. I'd always enjoyed her vivaciousness at showers, and what few family gatherings we'd manage to hit at the same time.

What I didn't know was that Vicki didn't know where I lived. She only knew the name of the street. But she told me that when she got behind the wheel of her car, she prayed her first audible prayer. She said, "If You want me to get right with You, You'll have to guide me there." She had determined in her heart to stop at every lit porch light until she had the right house, because she was crying so hard that she couldn't go back in the house to call.

She pulled right into our drive-way! And when I opened the door, expecting the same cover-up kind of mirth, a sobbing Vicki threw herself into my arms! I just held her for a few moments while the Holy Spirit prepared her heart for that which He was about to do, then led her into the living room where she cried out to God, and turned her life over to Him.

Then, she wanted to know about the baptism of the Holy Spirit, and as I turned to more scriptures she said, "I want all that He has for me." She bowed her head and received the Holy Spirit with such sweet sincerity and openness—oh, what a joy!

(How could anyone ever say, "I led So-and-So to Christ" when God does it all?)

We had such a precious time talking and sharing, far into the night. She said she felt as though a "thousand pound weight had dropped off" of her. She also mentioned that she had some friends that were seeking—could she bring them over sometime?

She did.

There were two the next night—praise God—and one the night after!

We had such a great time, I was almost afraid to get well! They all had such a hunger to have more of the Lord. They knew their lives lacked power. But the sad thing was the comment that they made—that "we can't find anyone who can help us. There are so few who want to talk about Jesus."

And now you can see why charismatics get into so much trouble. Two of these women were members in other churches. What is one supposed to say? That I could not ethically point them to what their heart needed, because it would look as though we were trying to get them into *our* church? That there was an answer to the need of their heart— but their pastor might be displeased with them when they found the satisfaction they were look-ing for? Could I tell them their decision might mean rejection? ridicule? I told them that that might be part and parcel of what they would be getting themselves in for—but their hearts were so hungry to have more of the Lord—it made no difference to them. And the joy and radiance on their faces was reward enough for me—indeed, a confirmation that I had done what was right.

To have stopped Vicki from coming here that night would have been like trying to stop a baby from being born! God IS building a house, and He's building it His own way!

More later—
Char

LETTER TWENTY-ONE

Dearest Lennie,

I don't see how a house can burn down so quickly when I can't even get one independent log to burn enthusiastically in my fireplace! I'm becoming famous in the neighborhood for my two-candle watt fire. Gene just came in to rescue me and is undertaking in the fire-building department.

He said, "How could anyone who thought for years that firemen shinnied back UP the pole *after* the fire be expected to know how to *start* one?"

But I don't have any trouble at all starting a fire in my oven! Last Christmas day, my sister Lauraine and I nearly died of hysterics. The juice from a pie caught fire in the oven and we were doing everything we could do in the kitchen to keep the charred odor from reaching our Auntie's delicate nostrils in the living room! We were covered from top to bottom with white, because we knew there was something "white" you were supposed to put oven fires out with, so we threw everything "white" we could get our hands on—salt, soda, flour. I said

I was the only person I knew who had to clean their oven out with a snow shovel!

I doubt if I'd have any new solutions for fire-fighting for an old pro like you. But Lennie, let me tell you how the Lord fought a fire for *us!*

It was a year or so ago. It was a misty, rainy Sunday evening. We were sitting in our beloved "warehouse" where we hold our meetings. Suddenly, we heard sirens coming from every direction. (The sky had had such an eerie look, anyhow. We were all a bit unsettled, as it brought back unpleasant memories of the violent tornado we'd experienced a few years ago.)

I got so uncomfortable, inside. Somehow, I knew we were vaguely connected again with those sirens.

A few minutes later, someone came to the door, asking for Gene and me. They came to tell us that our store was in great danger, as the rubber manufacturing plant that was situated right behind the store was in flames and completely out of control. Along the entire back side, our store was only six feet away from the rubber factory!

The fellowship began to pray, and we raced to the fire—took one look at the flames that were licking over the store, and our hearts sank.

"It's hopeless!" cried Gene. How my heart ached. It would mean utter ruin for him.

By now the area was impassable due to fire trucks, hoses, unbearable heat and mass confusion. Frantically, Gene helped them break one of the huge plate glass windows so that merchandise could be carried out, hoping to salvage at least some of it.

I remember feeling a bit numb. This business had been my enemy at one time. But now, it meant much to me. I went to a neighbor's house across the street and asked if I could slip into a room by myself. They were so absorbed in the fire, I guess they didn't even think it sounded strange. And there, I gave it all to the Lord, and began to praise Him for what He was about to do —assuring Him that all we had was His, and if this was His way of re-arranging our lives, we would thank Him and praise Him for the opportunity of showing the world that a loss like this could be taken in stride, when one knows the Lord. And then I spent some time praying in the Spirit. I walked down stairs and glanced across the street expecting to see the store in flames—only to observe people looking and pointing at the sky—BECAUSE THE WIND HAD CHANGED—AND THE FLAMES WERE REACHING FAR OUT THE OTHER WAY, ACROSS THE TRACKS WHERE THERE WERE NO HOMES!

Oh, Lennie! There wasn't even a paint blister on our store!. (The entire rubber manufacturing plant burned to the ground.)

We wanted to thank everyone who had done so much for us so we submitted this word of thanks to the paper:

117

CARD OF THANKS

Potterbaum's Appliance City wishes to thank all firemen and those who helped to save our store on Sunday, Aug. 22. We wish also to acknowledge those who fought the fire "on their knees" for we feel that a sovereign God shifted the wind and put us out of danger. Also, a tremendous thanks to the two neighbors across the street who allowed us to use the water from their swimming pools. Without the working co-operation of all, we would have faced utter ruin. Because our gratitude is so great, we would even be happy to service the sets that were "carried off" when merchandise was carried out of the store! Our heartfelt thanks to all.

Potterbaum's

Now, isn't Jesus wonderful!

Love—
Char

LETTER TWENTY-TWO

Dear Lennie,

Oh, that wonderful Name of Jesus! Praise that Holy Name—and oh, that Name is still as powerful as it was in Jesus' day!

I just came back from Vicki's, and I'm about to bubble over into the waste-basket because Jesus just proved to us that His glorious Name is still the mightiest force there is available to us!

She called me about lunchtime. She'd been plagued with a pain in her head, tingling in arms and legs and a general feeling of disinterest in spiritual things altogether, for about two weeks, since she'd returned from a visit to her parents' home down in Texas.

I hated to see her like this because she'd been doing so well, spiritually. But she'd been doing a lot of effervescent witnessing for Jesus, and I could see why Satan would like to put her out of commission for a time.

Well, she'd called and asked me to come over and pray for her. So, I walked into her house, dispensed with any small talk and dutifully laid my hands upon her and prayed in obedience to Mark 16:18—the verse the fundamentalists don't quite know what to do with. (In Mark it says "They shall lay hands on the sick, and they shall recover.")

Nothing happened.

She looked just as miserable and joyless as when I walked in.

I said, "Vicki, have you been praising the Lord?"

Listlessly she said, "Char, I can't. I don't even want to." She then went on to say some things that made me rather suspicious—like not caring whether she ever went to another meeting—how she didn't enjoy the vacation she'd taken because she didn't want to talk to anyone at her mother's —how she hadn't been herself . . .

Then she said something that gave me a key . . .

She said, "I've felt this way ever since I drove over that bridge. That horrible, long frightening bridge. I have never been so paralyzed with fear in my whole life . . . I've been so afraid of dying since then . . . didn't you tell me that Christians shouldn't fear death? I know I'm saved and shouldn't fear it, but last night I was so afraid of dying . . ." her voice trailed off.

I said, "Vicki! That's it! Don't you see? A spirit of fear capitalized on your panic when you crossed that bridge! Remember how I told you I had problems when we came home from Rome? How I didn't want to hear anything about Jesus, or the baptism with the Holy Spirit, or about the fellowship? It was as though it wasn't me at all doing my own thinking! And it *wasn't!* When Lynn prayed for me and commanded the spirit of unbelief to leave, it *did!* And I was free! I cried like a baby —it was such an awful feeling to be gripped by such a thing! Close your eyes—we're going to pray again!"

But I didn't close *my* eyes! I looked right at her and said, "In the Name of Jesus, I command you to come out! Spirit of fear, you MUST depart in the Name of Jesus. He has given me this authority, and YOU MUST LEAVE!"

She dropped her head into her hands and began to sob deep wretching sobs combined with some coughing.

I waited. . . .

And when she looked up at me, very slowly she took a deep breath—looked around the room almost dazed, somewhat. And then, oh, praise the Lord! She said "Char—I'm free! Oh, I can laugh again! The pain is gone! Oh, it's too *good* to be true!"

She got up, walked across the floor and burst out laughing! She said, "Hallelujah? I can praise Him again! Oh, I feel so great!" and she put her hands together and did a silly little dumb leap that made us both laugh, but must have been just as much an offer of worship as King David came up with umpteen centuries ago.

I had to get home to cook supper, so I left— but oh, how our hearts were singing! As I drove home, I laughed delightedly because I remembered

121

reading in Luke 11:20 where the Lord said, "But if I with the finger of God cast out devils, no doubt the kingdom of God is come upon you."

I laughed, because He did it as effortlessly as you or I would flick a bread-crumb from off the table—with our finger! One little nudge of the finger of God and it had to depart because of that wonderful Name.

I know there are people declaring up and down that a Christian can't have a demon, and I'm not quite sure I care to get in on the argument—but this one thing I know—if the need arises and someone is being gripped by terrible fear, paralyzing jealousy, or any one of the number of names these foul spirits go by—I am not about to argue doctrinally as to who "can" and who "cannot" be plagued with a demon. He has put the power at our disposal . . . and it works!

Glory!

Lennie, don't think for a moment that these wonderful things are happening just to Gene and me! We know of many saints who are being used as vessels for the Lord. They could ALL write books! It's just that these experiences are OUR experiences, so they are the ones WE shout about!

Bye now—
Char

LETTER TWENTY-THREE

Dear Lennie,

I can't help chuckling when I remember the old "door-to-door" routine. I remember how we would go dutifully out on Tuesday nights and invite people to come to Sunday School—how we were told we had "no need to be afraid"—just tell them they are welcome and invite them to come. And be sure to comment on something that means a lot to them, like their pets, their decor, or maybe even their sweet children. And don't forget the bulletin—be sure to leave a bulletin.

Oh, Lennie, that's not God's way at all! You just can't confine the Holy Spirit to a schedule!

Listen to what's been going on here the last few weeks.

Jan and Terry (her fiance) had a big fuss.

I'd seen a growing hunger in Jan's eyes when she heard us talk about the Lord, so I knew that it couldn't be too long before she would get "zapped."

Sure enough. The "big fuss" was just the nudge

He needed to drive her to Himself. Truly, "all things work together for good. . . ."

So my beautiful little girl received the Holy Spirit and "went on her way rejoicing."

A few days later, I got a phone call from her.

"Mom, Karen's in bad shape. Give her all you've got—she's ripe and ready—she wants the Lord, Mom, and we're on our way over now." (And it wasn't even Tuesday night.)

In came a tearful Karen. I am not free to talk about her problem, but I sure am free to tell you about the answer *to* her problem. His name is Jesus, and He became her Savior just moments after she came through the door.

Well, Karen was enjoying her new relationship with the Lord. But something happened. She had trouble "hanging in there." Only after a couple of weeks, she realized that walking with the Lord was a bit more difficult than she had imagined.

She said, "I go with the old crowd, but I'm no longer happy with them. And, yet, I can't seem to really 'get with' this Jesus business—although something within me really wants to. I want to live a good, clean life, but it's like there is an awful struggle going on inside. And confusion—my mind seems to be so full of confusion. Can you help me?"

And with this, we told her about the baptism in the Holy Spirit, and how it "cements" the relationship and gives the power we need in our lives to keep us walking in the light.

Jan and I exchanged teary-eyed glances as we felt the room fill with Jesus' presence and He met Karen as Baptizer in the Holy Spirit. From a heart full of sincerity, Karen asked for the Holy Spirit and then graciously and tearfully thanked Him. Her eyes were sparkling and her mind was absolutely clear when she got up from her knees.

She laughed and hugged us both (one of the other signs of this baptism of love—you have to hug and kiss everything in sight!) and said, "Fifteen minutes ago I was all muddled and now I'm free! All those 'problems' are gone!"

I left them in Jan's room to laugh and cry together, while I went back to my task I'd started before—potato peeling. It had seemed like a pretty mundane task until Karen came in on the third potato.

Now, to all appearances, this would be enough to make any "dorm mother's" day. But it was only the beginning.

At 11:30 that same night, I got a phone call from Jan—again all teary-eyed—crying, "Mom—it's Terry!"

"Sweetheart, is he hurt?"

"Mom, no! He just accepted Christ and asked for the Holy Spirit, and—oh—Mom, we're so happy . . . I mean he's so happy . . . we're all crying, Mom . . ."

"Honey, who's 'we' and where are you? And please do blow your nose!"

"We're here at Ron's apartment. Terry had to

125

come and wake him up and tell him about Jesus—
and also to tell him he loves him, and that he was
sorry he'd treated him so badly yesterday—he really
was short with him—and, Mom! Ron says he wants
what Terry has. Can you and Dad come right
over—and bring your Bibles—and—hey, Mom,
sorry about not being in by 11:00—that same
Holy Spirit you can't keep on a schedule must be
on Eastern Standard Time—Hurry, Mom."

Well, needless to say, we had a prayer and praise
meeting like you've never seen, and it wasn't even
"prayer meeting" night!

Lennie, there is nothing like it! The Holy Spirit
is preparing hearts all around us, and truly the
harvest is ready. Jan's only been filled with the
Spirit for three weeks, and she is already being
used to bring a crop in!

Even Mark and Jamie have been in on the excitement.

Jamie came in to pilfer the cookie jar and
matter-of-factly stated that his friends, Peter and
Jeff, had asked Jesus to come into their hearts.

"Jamie, how did that happen?" (I was elated!)

Jamie (only six) nonchalantly announced, while
picking the nuts out of the chocolate chip cookies,
"Easy, we just told them that you ask Jesus to come
into your heart—and when you felt a big 'bump'—
He was in."

What a shame that we adults clutter the whole
experience up with intellect, fear, arguments, and
shame. Oh, for the simplicity of children.

Well, haven't had my overdose of chocolate for the day, and I see one of the kids has prepared me a fudge sundae . . . wouldn't want to break their hearts or anything, so I'll go have another stab at gastric acidity.

Love,
Char

LETTER TWENTY-FOUR

Dear Lennie,

Now I know what they mean by hoarse-power. Whatever did the apostle Paul do without a telephone? I've had young wives and mothers pounding my ear for several days, but they've been using little trip-hammers of joy, zeal, and enthusiasm, so it's not at all hard to take.

Especially Judy.

She just called to tell me that the Lord had poured so much blessing out on her, she wasn't quite sure she could handle it. Now I know this is just like the Lord, but this sure isn't what Judy has always been like.

I can hardly believe it's been only three months since we faced each other over forgotten coffee cups as I listened almost disbelieving to her "story."

I had never seen her before this time. The pastor had given her my name as we were in the same neighborhood, so she had called and asked if she could come over.

She started her conversation something like this:

"Well, I can only tell you that I hate my housework, I can barely stand my kids, and I'm not too crazy about my husband. Two nights ago I repeated a bunch of words in front of your pastor and my brother, and now they say I am a Christian. How can I be when I feel so hateful, mean and miserable? To be real honest with you, I don't even want to go on living!"

And *I* was supposed to tell her how to find happiness on the backside of the desert?

Well, as the Lord promised, the Holy Spirit led me to say at least a few things that seemed to minister to her needs. She seemed to find enough satisfaction in the conversation to want to establish some kind of a relationship, and I was happy for this. I kept thinking over some of the details of her life (she didn't leave a thing out), and I wondered why people wait so long before they cry out to the Lord. I'd have cried out to Him for mercy many an episode ago, had I been in her shoes.

Two days later I got a frantic phone call from her mother. "Judy's in a terrible way—can you go to her? I'm at work, but even if I were free to go, I wouldn't know what to say to her. She sounded so desperate—can you go?"

I was putting on my coat before she even said good-bye. A love for Judy had tugged at my heart since we'd met, and by the time I left the house I was properly mad with the devil for raising such

129

havoc, and decided to wipe him up with a whole lot of Jesus talk, and chase him right out of that house!

I knocked at her door. It took her such a long time to get to the door, I began to think I might already be too late. When she finally came to the door she was much too groggy from far too many sleeping pills.

Lennie, such a sad dissheveled bit of humanity. Her eyes were swollen from long hours of weeping. She looked pale, gaunt and hollow-eyed. I could see she didn't want to talk to anyone. I was tempted to make it look as though I was passing by and had decided to drop in, but that would have bordered on being deceitful, so I stated my case squarely.

I said, "Judy, I know you'd rather see an angel of death, but the Lord has sent me instead via a frantic phone call from your mother. Where's your coffee pot? We both need some."

And I charged right through her house as though I were welcome.

I guess she decided she was too weary to put up a fight. She slumped into the chair opposite me and began to weep. She kept saying she couldn't go on—she was going to have her doctor put her in the "psych" ward at the hospital.

"Over my Living Bible, you will!" I exclaimed.

She seemed to think it was the only answer as she "had to get away." I didn't really want to encourage her to run from her problems, but I kept

130

getting another idea that just couldn't be batted out of my mind. As we talked, I made the pleasant discovery that she knew Beth quite well and that they had run around together as teenagers. It occurred to me that Beth's cheeriness might give her a lift, so we called Beth in Florida. As she shared with Judy, I could see a little spark of interest as Beth told her how bad things had been between her and Bert, and of how graciously the Lord had come in and healed over these hurts and removed the hostilities.

After she hung up she said wistfully, "I'd love to see Beth again."

I said, "There's your answer! We are flying down to be with them one month from today, plus take in a great teaching seminar in Miami. You said you needed to get away—come with us!"

I had a few qualms because I didn't like encouraging a wife to leave her husband for any length of time, but I felt the time had come when a little dose of homesickness would do both parties a lot of good.

She said, "To *Florida?*"

"Well, I don't plan on getting hi-jacked anywhere *else!*" I sputtered.

So away we went, bag, baggage and Bible to Beth, Bert, and the Christian Growth Conference. What a change it made in Judy! She'd asked for the baptism before she left, but she didn't receive her prayer language until she was alone in her bedroom in Florida. It blessed her so! She had opportunities to witness to relatives there, which helped to strengthen her faith. She began to realize there was something worth living for after all. She found herself getting very homesick for that little family back home, as healing love began to flow through her to others.

You see, this was Judy's second marriage, which always complicates inter-personal relationships. But as she began to experience the love of God, she had a great desire to be obedient to the Word. She knew it would mean making this marriage "work." She knew it would mean being done with little girl attitudes and tantrums. She knew it wasn't going to be easy—but the challenge appealed to her.

When she first came to talk and mentioned divorce, I didn't look the least bit shocked, but told her she should go ahead. She could do it the world's way if she so chose. But I told her that those feelings of guilt would be multiplied many times over . . . and though it was a quick, easy solution . . . it only opened the way for more sorrows. Then I told her if she would try God's way, it would be hard and bumpy, but so full of blessing, she wouldn't be able to contain it all.

Well, here she was telling me that on the phone. I wondered if she had recalled my saying that God would fill her so full she wouldn't be able to contain it . . . but somehow it didn't seem important whether she remembered it or not. Her love for

Christ had made her circumstances not only quite tolerable, but quite enjoyable.

It was just a few days after we'd come home from Florida when Judy said, "Char, I'm making the beautiful discovery that I CAN be happy, if I will just let myself BE happy!"

And I can't help getting all tickled pink on the inside, because as a young girl—besides desiring to write—I'd always had a hankerin' to be a MARRIAGE COUNSELOR!

Got to go grocery shopping, so . . .

More later,
Char

P.S. The night we got back from Florida, Judy's son accepted the Lord and the baptism of the Holy Spirit; a month later her husband came into the same experience, and three weeks later her sister was gloriously baptized in the Spirit!

LETTER TWENTY-FIVE

Dear Lennie,

Don and Barb will be here soon to talk over some more plans about the wedding. Oh, Lennie, it seems like only yesterday when he and your Cindy were traipsing off to kindergarten together. I remember how we laughed when Gene said if the teacher asked him his name, he'd probably say, "Donnie-Don't." But now that the role of mother-in-law is fast upon me, I must be done with "Donnie don'ts." He and Barb will have to make their own decisions and face their own mistakes— without mother's "Donnie don'ts."

And Jan and Terry set a date to get married just after they got themselves all straightened out with the Lord. I can see a newer, different kind of love replacing the old, somewhat demanding, possessive love they had for one another, and it's a precious thing to see.

When they came to talk it over with us, we had to admit that we felt the problem was not so much with early marriages as with marriages without

Christ as the foundation. (Jan is 18 and Terry is 20.) So we gave them our blessing, and I tried not to be too alarmed at the thought of two weddings four weeks apart.

Jan is really excited because today she witnessed her first glimpse of what is called "Holy Matrimony." (To call the experience just a wedding would not do it justice.) Today, our Woody and Bonnie got married. They are two kids from Zion Chapel fellowship. My heart was nearly bursting with love for these two when I saw them standing beneath a twining candlebra looking at one another as the brothers and sisters from Zion sang softly, "I love you, and you love me, His banner over us is love. . . ."

I didn't have a lump in my throat because of the beauty of the setting or the beauty of the bride, although Bonnie was very beautiful—but because of the faithfulness of God, as there is quite a story behind these two.

I first became aware of Woody because I saw the joy of the Lord all over his face. I watched him from a distance for a number of meetings, smiling when our eyes met, and thinking to myself how young and handsome he was.

And then he came up to me one day and said, "Did I hear someone call you Mrs. Potterbaum?"

"Yes. Why do you ask?" (I could see he was stifling a snicker.)

"Well—I don't exactly know how to tell you

this—I don't know—maybe I shouldn't, but . . . well, anyhow, does your husband have the appliance store here in town?"

"Ye—es, I can see you're about to choke on that chuckle. Out with it! What are you trying to say?" We were both laughing happily now with just the sheer joy of the Spirit.

Cautiously, he began. "Well, I don't know how you're going to take this, but my "former" friends and I bought one of your used dryers to "dry" our "grass" in."

"Oh, *no!* . . . Woody, where is it now?" I roared. (Somehow this struck me as hilarious.)

"At the sheriff's . . . they used it for evidence."

And then I found out more of the particulars. It seems Woody had served time for "growing grass" (marijuana) but through a real "twist of fate" (at least in the eyes of most people) he hadn't had to serve the full sentence, which I think was two years. Woodie would be the first to acknowledge the Lord in the whole incident. Shortly after he was free, he started coming to our prayer meetings and found in the first meeting what he'd been searching for during those hectic rebellious years. He was saved, delivered and filled with the Spirit at the first meeting he attended!

That was about one year ago. I couldn't help thinking how fine he looked, how happy and secure in his love for Christ and in the love of his glowing bride, Bonnie.

And then I must tell you something about Bonnie. She had come from a wonderful home and a real fine Christian background. But Bonnie had something that was bothering her very much. She was a beautiful girl, but had been plagued with an unusually bad complexion. Since she was very sensitive, it had always caused her much concern.

One particular night, a brother from Wales came to speak to us. This brother had been given the "word of knowledge" (I Corinthians 12:8). The word of knowledge is one of the nine gifts of the Spirit given to the Church for the uplifting of its members (the body).

So just after the message, when the Lord's blessing was hanging heavy in the air, and hearts were very tender, the brother from Wales prayed and then quietly made this comment.

"Just before the meeting, someone here looked into the mirror at home and had a heavy heart because of a fear that the problem you are having with your complexion would leave pits and scars. The Lord has impressed it upon me to tell you that there will be no pits or scars, and that He loves you."

I couldn't help thinking of that when I saw how radiant Bonnie was—and how absolutely lovely her complexion was.

Oh, Lennie, He cares so very much about even the smallest things in our lives!

I wish you could have heard the wedding ceremony. It was *not* traditional. You see, Christ was the Central One, not the bride. There was a sermon that not only spoke to the bridal couple, but to every married couple there. The message of the sermon was submission—to one another, to brothers and sisters in Christ, to pastors—and with exhortations to continually think of fulfilling the needs of the "other one" as a means of bringing happiness to yourself . . . that sowing love and unselfishness *reaps* love and unselfishness.

I have a feeling Woody and Bonnie's relationship will be more meaningful than the one I heard of last week. A new bride I know (who doesn't know the Lord yet) was so upset with her husband that she made *only her side of the bed!* That's better known as rebellion in action!

More later.

Love,
Char

LETTER TWENTY-SIX

Dear Lennie,

My life used to be so simple! Nothing but diapers and formulas to worry about. Now we've entered into the stage of co-signing and mortgage arrangements for the up-and-coming, now-voting generation that still has to have parents' signatures to sneeze!

You should have seen me at the bank. A kind man sat across the desk from us explaining the world of interest, taxes, percentages and so on. I tried desperately to look intelligent, but when he glanced my way and said, "Do you understand?" I could only smile weakly and admit that I couldn't even double a recipe without an abacus. He seemed quite surprised when I came up with a full signature instead of an "X". And for once, Don was glad I *hadn't* used my maiden name.

Watching these kids begin new lives with new mates and new responsibilities can be both scary and exciting. I feel such concern—have I prepared them well enough for the hurts that are ahead . . . the inevitable problems that will crop up?

139

Are they prepared to accept the faults in their mates that young love has blinded them to . . . faults that are there because they are human and imperfect? Will they have the quality of character that will be willing to admit their own deficiencies? Will I be a help—or a hindrance?

And so our lives unfold, one strand at a time.

I wish I could see Larry entering into this kind of an adventure.

I haven't said much about Larry thus far because he is so close to my heart. You do remember him, don't you?

Larry doesn't live here anymore. Larry, of the artistic nature . . . Larry, the nostalgic one . . . Larry, the mysterious one . . . my eldest . . . my son.

Larry loved the Lord at one time . . . he even felt God was calling him to be an evangelist.

What made him change? Who's to say?

Lennie, he has so much going for him. He has such a terrific wit! Listen to some of the things he wrote home from basic training:

"Dear Mom and Dad, I'm so sore. Five minutes ago I started to sneeze, and my stomach muscles are still recoiling. Maybe I won't look any different to you when I get home, but I've done so many push-ups, I'll bet I could pick up a dime with my navel. Today we got our M-16's. Can't shoot it yet, but I can squish cockroaches with the butt real good!"

No, Larry doesn't live here anymore.

He's off "doing his own thing." And someday, that wonderful heart of his that has always been so great at sharing the hurts of others will beat in accord with my Lord, and Larry will find the place he was always meant to have . . . close to the heart of God.

Lennie, he is so much like me. One of the reasons we always clashed was because I saw all of my own weaknesses in him. It makes me so sad to think that he had to bear the brunt of all my immaturities. But with all our differences, there has always been a deep love between us.

Someday, Lennie, prayerfully soon, I'll be tapping a letter out to you that reads, "Lennie! My Larry loves my Jesus now!" And the angels will be doing so much rejoicing you'll be able to hear them!

Well, it's time to bundle the brood off to bed. I just found Jamie holding a shirt up to himself in the mirror—I thought, "Isn't that wonderful? He's beginning to care about what looks well together," so I said, "What's up, Jamie?"

He didn't even look my way. He just mumbled, "Nothin'. Just tryin' to see how far up I'll have to wash."

Never a dull moment around here.

More later.

Char

LETTER TWENTY-SEVEN

Dear Lennie,

What do wedding bells mean to me? A couple of ding-a-lings bumping into each other while coming and going! And at one time I thought those two ding-a-lings *loved* me. Now I'm convinced they are out to *get* me!

At every turn it's, "Mom, do you really need this old thing anymore?" as one of them picks up some treasured antique.

Or, "Hey, that would look great on my stereo . . ." and poof! It's gone. I've taken to using epoxy glue generously on the bottom of anything that would match their decor.

As we were hosting at Don's rehearsal dinner I nudged Gene and pointed to the sea of faces before us. Twenty-three, in fact.

"Do you see all these people?" I whispered. "Do you realize that if our kids all marry—that's six more—and if they have only two kids—and if we live through all those weddings—we will be a total of 26—every Easter, Christmas, New Year's, Thanksgiving, etc.?"

It was almost as traumatic as when I tallied up the number of nails that had to be trimmed and cared for—160 in all—plus 16 ears, and 56 pairs of sox, all needing mates—until high boots came in.

Well, I'm happy to tell you that both weddings are now past history. The Bible says a man is to leave his father and mother and cleave unto his wife. Only thing—I didn't remember it hurting so much when they cut the umbilical cord the first time.

And for the life of me, I can't see why a couple of twenty minute ceremonies should take six months of preparation. But they did.

Jan tried her wedding dress on for her father a few days before the wedding. Naturally, I got all misty-eyed as she walked slowly from us, turning gracefully so that the train and all the lacy finery curved about her slender form.

I blubbered for a minute and said, "Oh, sweetheart! You look like . . . like a beautiful white . . ."

"Try dollar sign" interjected her father as he was looking over the bills for the wedding. He was going over the itemized list from the florist.

He said, "Lanterns? They're carrying lanterns? *Candle*-lit lanterns?"

"Yes," I said, "flower bedecked, at that" as I helped to arrange her gown about her just for the fun of it. I saw him run his finger carefully up and down the list.

I said, "What are you looking for?"

He sighed, "Hopefully, a flower bedecked fire extinguisher for *me* to carry! I'd feel a lot safer if Smokey the Bear was giving her away. And speaking of giving away . . . when they ask 'who giveth this woman?' I think I'll say '*giveth*, my foot!' and whip out all these itemized bills!"

Jan said, "*Daddy*" in her most grown up tone. And then he smiled to let her know that he wasn't serious, that he loved her so much, he didn't mind.

Oh, Lennie, this is what life is all about . . . change and adjustment . . . no two days ever being alike. Happy occasions—and trying not to think about sad ones, but knowing full well they are a part of life, too.

Love,
Char

LETTER TWENTY-EIGHT

Dear Lennie,

A few pages ago I spoke musingly about these letters becoming a book. God is so big, and so far ahead of us—why does He continually put up with our shortsightedness?

It all started down in Florida. Gene and I had gone down there for the Christian Growth conference and also to spend some time with Beth and Bert.

What a week! We soaked up teaching given out by brothers Mumford, Baxter, Prince and Basham. It was a thrill to hear them speak as Gene and I had read most of their books.

During lunch break one day, I decided I'd ask one of these brothers what I should do with my manuscript. With much bravado, I stepped up to one of the brothers, touched his sleeve, and mentioned—from a very dry throat—that I had a partial manuscript—did he have any suggestions?

Immediately I was sorry I had even asked because I suddenly realized I didn't fit the picture of an authoress—AT ALL! My inferiorities came rushing in to second the vote . . . and Satan whispering in my ear, "You dum-dum! You've never published *anything!* And your first rejection came from the *church bulletin!*"

But the brother was very polite and didn't yawn or scratch his head like most people do when I mention my desire to write. He just looked at me and said, "Send it to Whitaker's. If it has any merit, they will see it."

After the afternoon session, we spotted Wes Smith. He too, was an author. We hadn't seen him since he'd left Zion Chapel territory, so after many questions and a few hugs, we decided to go have coffee. Suddenly, in the middle of a sentence, Wes leaned toward me and said "Charlene, Whitaker's is looking for new authors. Didn't you say you had an idea for a manuscript?"

I mumbled something into the fudge sundae I shouldn't have been eating, to the effect that well, yes, but I didn't know if it was any good or not—and wished desperately I'd never mentioned it to *anyone!*

Then, on our first Sunday home, Dean, who orders our books for us at church, came to me and said, "I see where Whitaker's is looking for manuscripts. Why don't you give them a whirl?"

I thought "Hm-m-m-m. In the mouth of two or three witnesses, Lord?" Could be!

So a few days later, I mustered up all the courage I had, picked up the phone and called Mr. Whitaker.

I can't help wondering how he ever had enough faith in my ability to finish a book when I had so little success with finishing a sentence! The conversation went something like this:

Mr. Whitaker: "Tell me about your book."

Frightened me: "It's about—well, you see, I thought—I like letters—I mean, it's all about letters—er, people—and things."

Patient Mr. Whitaker: "Could you tell me a little more, please?"

More frightened me: "I'd hoped to write—well, I mean—I wanted so to come up with something that would sink into people's hearts." (Finally, a whole sentence.) We talked for a few moments more. He was really quite nice. It's amazing how beginning authors can picture editors and publishers as absolutely ogre-ish!

He said, "Send me what you have. We'll look it over."

Pwhew! I was convinced I should have stayed with cookie-baking.

I started to fix supper. We had company coming, so I busied myself about the kitchen. The kids were outside—the house was empty. Then, something very beautiful happened. Putting it into words will be very difficult, but I must try because I so desire for God to receive the glory due Him.

Something welled up within me. It was a spiritual happening, a blessing, an energizing by the

Holy Spirit . . . an awareness that He was trying to tell me something.

I began to cry. Please forgive me, but I'm as happily weepy now as I used to be depressingly weepy. I said, "Lord? What is this?" And just as quickly, I realized it was the gift of faith! He was letting me know that Whitaker's was going to take my book—*our* book! That He was giving me the opportunity to declare His marvelous works to all the world! What an experience! I became enveloped in His love in a way I'd never known before.

The next day I dropped the partial manuscript into the mailbox. I experienced a peace that "passeth understanding." The kind of peace that is a product of being not only in His will, but in the very *center* of His will.

About three weeks later I got a call from Whitaker's—seems they had a question to ask me. Trying to sound calm, I said, "Tell me, when I hear your final decision, will it come by phone or by mail?"

She thought for a moment. "I'd imagine by mail. Why do you ask?"

"Oh, nothing. It's just my poor mailman. I think I kind of overwhelm him. I'm sure the old dear thinks I have a crush on him because I'm always waiting at the door for him, hoping he'll have some word on the manuscript. I'm afraid one of these days he'll start leaving my mail on the curb instead of coming up to the door. . . ."

She laughed and said, "You'll have word in a few days."

Well, I've since learned that if your publisher says "in a few days," it editorially means "this month or next."

A few more weeks went by. I called their office and left this message: "Dear Nancy: Forget the manuscript. I just ran off with the mailman! Love, Char."

Gene said, "You *didn't!* No wonder you haven't heard . . . they probably threw it away!" Sure wish he hadn't said that. I had a bad enough time fighting my vivid imagination as to the whereabouts of the manuscript. Once, I imagined someone was sopping up Coke with it. Once, I imagined it blowing out the window. I have since learned that publishers are very careful and considerate, praise the Lord.

Well, that wonderful day came when the gift of faith was proven to have been a valid experience. Not wanting to be responsible for any more strain on the mailman, Whitaker's called to tell me that they would be sending me a contract. And when it came, I didn't know whether to sign it or frame it!

The Lord just proves again that His promises are true. He says in Psalm 37:4, "Delight thyself also in the Lord; and he shall give thee the desire of thine heart." He has truly been my delight, my everything. So He honored my desires. What's more, He caused my desires to line up with His desires by being the very author *of* the desire!

Hallelujah!

Love,
Char

P.S. Oh, Lennie, the goodness of God. I almost forgot to tell you that He arranged for Beth and Bert to give their testimony of what God had done in their lives over a Miami TV station.

Lennie, we didn't know anything about the broadcast, or when it would be televised . . . but God arranged for it to be shown on the only Sunday we were in Florida that year! He is so full of pleasant surprises!

LETTER TWENTY-NINE

Dear Lennie,

I keep patting the kids on the head and telling them to go do something funny so I can write about it. They all give me that impossible look and groan, but sooner or later they are obliging me with material without even knowing it!

The other day they were carrying the groceries in. Mark saw the grocery list lying there, and being neater than the average kid, he scrunched it up into a ball and threw it into the waste basket.

Laurie leaped to the basket, grabbed the list and dramatically hugged it to her, holding her arm to her forehead in mock despair.

"Mark! How could you! Mother *wrote* that—it may be *valuable* some day!"

And he, picking up the fiasco tore at his shirt and begged my forgiveness.

What characters!

And Jamie—he doesn't let me down, either. He saw Gene writing out a check on Saturday night, and he said, "Whatcha' doin', Dad?"

Gene said, "I'm making out a check to the church."

Jamie looked puzzled and said, "You mean Mom's got a charge account there, too?"

How dull my life would be without them. For the most part, they are a real delight to us. But when the scrapping and bickering begins, I can't help thinking of how we must grieve the Lord when we treat brothers and sisters in Christ unkindly.

More and more I'm coming to appreciate the analogy that is seen between the church and the family.

Gene, as shepherd, represents Christ in our home. I am the chief over-seer, in charge of maintenance under him—like the elder. And they, bless their little frustrating hearts are the "congregation." Guess that's why we got such a large congregation —so we could more fully see what this is all about.

We have those who are zealous, those who are jealous. We have some who are pious, some who will try us. We have the proud and the loud, some on fire, some in the mire. But we love them all, and feel our responsibility to them keenly.

Just the other day I was talking with Gene about this business of reverence and how important it is. I was curled up beside him on the couch, and was stealing some glances at him from under his arm. The feeling of reverence I had for him was so pleasant—so God given, and so essential to romance. I couldn't resist asking a typically dumb question.

I said, "Honey, do you enjoy looking at me as much as I do you? I mean, do you get a good feeling?"

He thought a moment. "I never thought much about it. I love you, though. And methinks I'm about to get myself talked into a tight spot if I'm not careful."

I laughed and said, "Silly. But I'm thinking you don't feel 'reverence'—nor are you supposed to. The Bible tells the woman she is to 'reverence her husband.' He is only instructed to 'love her.' And so I'm wondering if a man can ever experience this same feeling—this feeling of reverence that comes with right relationships, and all that goes with it."

He said, "But doesn't all love have an essence of reverence to it?"

I thought awhile, then said, "I don't think so. I love the kids—but not necessarily 'reverently.' I think reverence has to do with the one over you in authority. No, I don't think you should feel the same when you look at me. Yours should be more of the love that feels protecting—and if I don't quit thinking out loud, you'll think I'm being preachy, huh?"

We concluded the conversation by deciding that God never intended for a man to fully understand how the mind of a woman works any more than a woman can ever understand how the mind of a man works. They are only to complement each other and become a "whole" in marriage—without ever expecting to understand what makes the "whole" thing work. And therefore the need for the Holy Spirit. He understands the "whole" while we only see in part. Amen.

Love,
Char

LETTER THIRTY

Dear Lennie,

"Unto the pure, ALL things are pure" (Titus 1:15).

But the Puritans—bless their pure hearts, got *so* pure they played right into the hands of Satan by thinking of sex as something evil and bad.

I'm not exactly an advocate for sex education in the schools, but I sure do advocate sex education *somewhere!*

All these thoughts are stirring around in my heart because of a talk I just had with a young frustrated mother of three. We'll need to give her a name, but not her own, for obvious reasons. So let's call her Angie.

Angie started the conversation something like this:

"All the romance has gone out of my marriage. I can hardly stand my husband! I don't like the way he walks—I don't like the way he sits, moves —everything he does irritates me to death. And he's starting to get FAT, and I hate Fat!"

I thought I'd ignore the last comment and

hoped she hadn't noticed how much I looked like a triple-decker ice cream cone as I leafed through the Bible to get some encouragement from brother Paul's words to Titus. I felt the time had come to move into that somewhat uncomfortable area in Titus where Paul says "The AGED women. . . ." (I've wished many a time that the dear King James' translators would have been a bit more tactful and said something like "vine-ripened" or "more mature") . . . "may teach the young women to be sober, to love their husbands, to love their children . . . to be keepers at home . . . obedient to their OWN husbands," etc.

Obviously, God knew there would be days like this and problems like this, or He wouldn't have instructed us to be prepared. What's more, these are not just modern day frustrations but a need that the Holy Spirit was able to see down through the ages as the Epistle was written by Paul sometime before his second imprisonment about the year 67 A.D.

My heart really ached for Angie. A marriage that has gone "cold" is as disheartening as is the Christian life when *it* has grown cold. I had a firm belief that God intended for love to bloom and flourish and continue growing WITHIN a marriage just as surely as he intended for our love for Him to blossom and grow.

But love could not grow where all of these bad heart attitudes had cropped up unhindered. I was certain she had loved her husband very much when she married him. As we talked, I toyed with the idea of handing her a book on how to have a radiant marriage, but I knew she would wind up hating her husband at about page twenty-six, because he didn't do ANY of the prescribed things for a happy marriage! He was one of these contented fellows that was completely oblivious to the needs of his wife. He provided well for his family, and was patient with the children. I'm sure he'd think, "What else could a woman ask?" No doubt he had somewhere rambled off into that Never-Never land of indifference so attainable to so many males—a land perfectly suited for growing hostilities in its fertile soil.

From having dealt with a number of young mothers with like problems and attitudes, I thought I knew of another area that was probably distasteful to her. I let her talk for awhile, then I said, "Angie, you have never had a fulfilling sex experience, have you?"

She was a bit startled and stammered around with a lot of "er's" and "well—uh's" until she finally admitted," "No." But she couldn't see what connection this had with her attitude towards her husband.

And this is where I needed God's wisdom. If I were to step in now and blurt something out about this whole thing being her husband's fault because he'd stopped "woo-ing" her—of how he'd never learned the importance of making the kind of love that leads to satisfying love-making in the bedroom, I'd only have her thinking less of him than when she walked in! No, I had only God's Word. And, as I fit the description of the (gulp) "aged woman," I could only pray that God would enable me to "teach" this young woman to "love" her husband. I thought if I used the same kind of caution that one would use when stringing a cactus with Christmas tree lights, the Holy Spirit would do the rest!

I said, "Angie, first of all—you need to see your husband through God's eyes. You need to change your attitude about him."

Her eyes began to fill with tears. "Oh, I really want to. I feel so rotten on the inside because of my attitude, but I can't seem to do anything about it!"

As we talked I was praying, "Lord, YOU must speak the necessary thing to her—help me to say it so that the Holy Spirit can bury it deep within her innermost being at just the right time."

I said, "Angie, the second thing you need to do is to pray about your sex prob—" But she interrupted me with, "Oh, NO!—I can't pray about THAT!" as though I had said something sacre-ligious!

I said, "Hold it! Hold it! . . . WHY can't you pray about it? Didn't the Lord Himself create the organs to function in their proper order? Isn't He the One who instituted this whole wonderful business of sex drives and attractions to the opposite sexes, and all THAT?"

And was I ever getting mad! Not at Angie, mind you. My whole being was reaching out to her with God's love—but I was so mad at Satan, I wanted to throw something! Maybe it's hard to understand how love and hate could be working in me at the same time, but I can only say that the deeper my love for Christ becomes, the more pure my hatred for Satan becomes!

And suddenly, I could see how we play into his hands.

We take the wedding ceremony and dress it up with finery and frills and insist on its being done in the church to have the sanction of God upon the public ceremony. Then we permit Satan to move in to the most secret place where the union becomes absolute and allow him to hold full sway in the hearts and lives of young people who have had no instruction or direction, simply because our society and churches have made a taboo out of frank but intimate discussion of such things.

So where are they going to learn? From the school playground, of course—just like you and I did.

You see, I feel there is such a beautiful parallel here—an unfolding of the "mystery" of Christ and His Church as spoken of in the Word when it says, "For this cause shall a man leave his father and mother and shall be joined unto his wife, and they two shall be one flesh. THIS IS A GREAT MYSTERY, BUT I SPEAK CONCERNING

CHRIST AND HIS CHURCH" (Ephesians 5:31–32).

I can't help but feel that some of this mystery is explained in this most holy of physical unions. Although every new bride has the POTENTIAL for a fulfilling sex experience, she does not usually experience this until she has been married awhile and learns to yield herself more completely to her husband. If he is tender, considerate, patient and loving, she comes into this experience much sooner. If he becomes indifferent, absorbed in his own interests, and callous to her emotional needs, then she will take much longer—perhaps many years before a fulfilling sex experience becomes hers experientially. But once she experiences this, there is a "bonding"—a greater intimacy. A deeper, more satisfying love.

Well, as Angie and I freely discussed these things, she became willing to admit that yes, perhaps she could pray about her sex problem.

But then she said, "But what *can* I do about my attitude towards my husband? He irritates me so!" And exasperation was written all over her face.

I said, "Angie, let's back up a few verses." (We still had our Bibles open to Eph. 5.) "Read verse 22 for me."

Slowly she read "Wives, submit yourselves unto your own husbands, as unto the Lord."

I said, "There is your key—AS UNTO THE LORD."

160

She said "I'm not quite sure of what you're trying to tell me. . . ."

I said "Angie—our husbands are the representatives of Christ in our homes. When God sees your husband, He sees him as the visible representation of Christ in your home. He also sees that what is done for your husband is the same as done to Christ. Everytime we express dissatisfaction with our husbands, we are expressing dissatisfaction with the Lord. When we are surly and ungrateful to our husbands, we are being surly and ungrateful to the Lord. You've heard it said that if we give even a cup of cold water in His Name, he counts it as having been given to Him. So, when we allow our hearts to come into a submissive attitude towards our husbands, we are submitting in the fullest sense to Jesus Christ! You have no idea how many dear women are whirling around in spiritual circles longing to get on with the Lord, but refusing to submit to the one over them in authority because he "isn't spiritual," "is immature," "doesn't even know the Lord" (for this spiritual law holds true even if the husband isn't a Christian!)

"Angie, when you learn to see your husband through reverent eyes you will fall in love with him all over again. As your attitudes change, you will be giving the Lord a chance to speak to your husband through the "meek and gentle" spirit that you will develop. Now remember that the

161

Bible says they may be won "without a word." That means there is no room for preaching, nagging, or belittling.

"Of course you have to determine in your heart whether or not you WANT to be obedient to the Word. And here in the New American Standard Bible it speaks about their (husbands') observing your chaste and *respectable* behaviour. That means you are going to have to overlook his weight problem, and begin to think more of his good points, and less about his bad points."

About this time the door-bell rang, so we had to end our discussion. But I had seen enlightenment in her eyes when we talked about seeing our husbands as Christ in the home. She'd never considered this before. I felt she'd be able to see him through reverent eyes, and if she were obedient to the Word by becoming submissive and loving, even though she might have to endure a bit of quiet suffering from this "well-doing," eventually their sex problem would take care of itself.

Lennie, I can't help but feel there is a great need for consecrated people who are willing to make themselves available for open and intimate discussion of such problems. We've found out that if you pray and ask the Lord to be present, there is no embarrassment—no holding back in the discussion. Oh, I know the easiest way is to cram a "how-to" book into their hands and then change the subject quickly. But let's face it—*you can't ask a book questions!*

And while I'm on the subject, I think I should mention that I know of many couples who have had a most satisfying sex life—but still ended up in a divorce court simply because they had never developed mature attitudes in other areas of their lives! We have a parallel to that, too, in the spiritual realm. For I have known people who have received the baptism of the Holy Spirit, yet they have never gone on into "maturity" because they have not been obedient to the Word of God, thus establishing right attitudes within them. I'm realizing more and more that God is much more interested in our motives, our attitudes, and our reactions, than He is in our "works."

More later
Char

LETTER THIRTY-ONE

Dear Lennie,

It's gotten so every morning I have to declare "state your name, rank and cereal preference" because of the over-hanging cabinets that separate their heads from my view as they march into their respective niches at the kitchen bar. I spend several minutes praying in the Spirit trying to stave off the next onslaught of pinching, poking and provoking that seems to go with the morning doldrums. Somehow I can never get the maze of polka dots, plaids and stripes focused properly until just after the second cup of coffee.

I'd gotten the kids off to school, and Larry and I were working on our first cup of coffee when Larry's friend Buzzy came in. We'd known Buzzy for a number of years, but it had been some time since I'd seen him. He and Larry lived together when they were in college.

First, Buzzy asked how all the various members of the family were doing. You know—light, easy conversation so no one can get uncomfortable—

and no one can get "close." And that's all right, because Jesus is Lord.

And then he said, "How's Frank doing?"

Frank was one of the "hippy" kids that had come here for counseling.

I said, "Fantastic. He has a tender love for Christ that grows by leaps and bounds."

He nodded his head.

"Well," he continued "that's fine if it's what you want—but me, I like to smoke a little pot—and I don't think the government has the right to tell me whether it's illegal or not!" he said, defensively. "I mean—I like to get high once in awhile, and I don't see anything wrong with it."

I had the feeling he was buggin' for an argument.

"But Buzzy—doesn't a natural high—no, I take that back—a SUPERNATURAL high have some appeal to you? A 'high' where there need be no coming down? A 'high' that can satisfy your innermost needs?" I said, between sips of coffee.

He counter-parted with, "Oh, you see I know Him—in my own way."

"Well, wonderful Buzzy—then you must be reading His Word, because that's the very best way. . . ."

"Well now—I didn't exactly mean THAT way."

"But the Bible says that if we love Him, we will want to keep His commandments and one of those commandments is to feed on His Holy Word. Aren't you doing that?" I knew he could see the

165

amusement in my eyes, and he was taking it all good-naturedly.

"Well, no—but I don't exactly think of it that way. I mean, I pray—"

"You pray, but you don't read the Word? That's like saying you breathe, but you refuse to eat. You're a great kid, Buzzy, but you've never had a glimpse of the whole picture. You've never discovered the peace that comes from submitting to the authorities over you as a means of driving out the rebellion that makes up the "self" that governs you. And not just you, Buzzy. All of us have had to contend with the "self" that makes up our total being. We have all been faced with a choice —am I going to allow "self" to reign supreme? Or will I permit Christ to take over the "reigns"?

I poured more coffee.

"Buzzy, go ahead and smoke your pot, because I don't think the Lord is interested in taking away the only puny, artificial pleasure you have. I believe God could care less about what you smoke or what you don't smoke. His main concern is the root problem of rebellion holding full sway in your heart. That part of you that "reacts" when someone crosses your will. That "something" that rears up when you can't have your own way. I'd even be so bold as to say that His main mission is to stamp out rebellion in the hearts of His creatures—not just to change some of their habits.

Light began to dawn. "Yeah? Hey, that's heavy—I never heard of anything like that before. And

166

that sure doesn't fit me—I mean, I gotta do my own thing—and I don't like anyone telling me what to do. Wow, I'm not ready for what you got, I can see that. . . . But I sure never heard it put like that before."

I'd made an interesting mental note that Larry had walked out of the room during the discussion. His fear of being convicted in any area is almost more than he can handle.

And so, when the coffee pot was empty, they left.

Since then Larry and Buzzy have moved to Arizona. But guess who went with them to Arizona? The Holy Spirit, of course. Every day I pray that He will plead with them—woo them, love them all the way to Jesus. From the radio—billboards, when hitch-hiking—and someday, this discussion will bear fruit. For God has promised that His Word will not return unto Him void. Oh, I know I didn't actually quote Scripture to Buzzy. But His Word went forth—because He IS out to stamp out rebellion in those who will turn to Him. One could almost say it is the main theme of the Bible.

Lennie, please pray for my Larry and his friend Buzzy. Buzzy isn't his real name, but God will know who you are praying for. And maybe they won't be in Arizona when you pray—but God will know where they are—and He moves as His people pray!

Back later—
Char

LETTER THIRTY-TWO

Dear Lennie,

Wow! What a life!

I never know from one day to the next where I'll be!

In John 3.8 (Amplified) it says, "The wind blows (breathes) where it will: and though you hear its sound, yet you neither know where it comes from, nor where it goes. So it is with every one who is born of the Spirit."

And so, in essence, people who are born of the Spirit are liable to pop up 'most any place, 'most any time!

For instance—a few weeks ago I was feeling very blue and lonely. It had been necessary for Gene to be gone almost the entire month of January. I'd had a crushing experience on a particular day and was hoping he'd call so I could pour it all out to him. I needed him so! I'd spent the entire month feeling like a heart running around without a "head."

The telephone rang. God bless telephones.

On the other end was the kind voice that means more to me than any voice on earth.

"Praise the Lord, Sweetheart! How are things at home?"

The deluge began. My heart was about to break. Not only was he in sunny warm Florida, but I could hear my darling Beth's giggle in the background, and that just about did me in—and then he threw in the remark that he'd be going to see Kathryn Kuhlman the next night!

He broke into my undainty sniveling with, "Hey! Hold it! That's why I'm calling—I want you to hop on a plane and fly down here tomorrow morning."

"It's impossible!" I blubbered. "The house is a mess—no baby-sitter—washing's not done—I've been counseling people for two days straight. But I'm sure homesick to see you—tell me I can do it! Tell me it can be done! Oh, I want to come so badly!"

He said "Now listen. You take your directions from the Lord through me. Right?"

"Right!"

"So make the necessary phone calls and call me back and tell me what time you'll be here."

What a guy!

I began dialing sitters and airports while breathing out a quick, "Lord, if you are in this make everything run smoothly." (It was already 10 p.m.)

There was one flight available—and Howard and

Ellen said, "we'll be happy to stay with the kids—we'll be there first thing in the morning."

The Lord sent the necessary adrenalin into my veins, and I did the wash, straightened the house—had my hair done after I arrived there—and had the time of my life! We went to see Kathryn Kuhlman (a first for both of us—and what an experience!).

Then, on Thursday night we sat on the edge of our seats as we sat under the teaching of Bob Mumford.

And then, to top a great week off—just as we were coming out of the doughnut shop in Key Biscayne, we ran into Joan again.

We'd become acquainted with Joan, when Beth had spotted her on the beach the last time we were here and remarked that Joan was desiring to know about the Lord, and would we talk to her?

I said "Honey, I'm feeling about as spiritual as the Man O'Wars that are endangering the shore line! My head is killing me!" I was so busy nursing self-pity and thinking of my own needs, I wasn't sure I could even feel another's needs enough to care!

"But Gene looks like he is in great shape," I said. "Why not ask her if she would be willing to come to your house? Then we'll know if she means business with God, or not."

Well, Joan came. And she meant business, all right! What a joy! Gene was in great shape—and he did all the talking. She met Jesus there as her Savior and her Baptizer. And when we were through praying, my head-ache was gone.

So, meeting Joan again outside of the doughnut shop was a real joy. She had a great word for us about her son, too. Beth and Bert had led her son to Christ, but he'd turned away from the Lord and had gone back into drugs. Hard drugs. The shooting kind. He had had to spend a few nights in jail. While there, he watched two others undergoing the agonies of withdrawal. In the meantime, a band of people were praying that God would minister to her son in such a way that he would renew his fellowship with the Lord, and that God would spare him from going through withdrawal. He came back to the Lord, went to a Christian re-hab center, experienced no withdrawal symptoms, and has been "straight" ever since! Oh, Lennie, God is SO good!

Well, needless to say the short vacation was a real blessing. And when I got home, one more little "tid-bit" kinda topped the whole thing off.

It seems that Howard and Ellen had felt led of the Lord to give their last penny away on the night before I called them for "baby-sitting." Howard is a teacher, but his entire pay-check goes for bills and groceries, with so little left over.

And so they gave their "little left-over" to the Lord and looked to him for their needs. By coming to our house, they had free groceries for a

171

week—and the amount I paid them for their services would get them through until their paycheck came again in two weeks! You see, the Lord was "in it."

Bye now—
Char

LETTER THIRTY-THREE

Dear Lennie,

I've heard it said that there are many inspirational 3:16s in the Bible. I think today I just found my favorite, Leviticus 3:16 . . . "All the fat is the Lord's." So now I'm going to hold him to it!

All this time you've heard me talk about being twenty pounds overweight and making all those limp excuses all overweight people make. Well, in all honesty I must tell you that that twenty pounds has swelled to thirty pounds, and try as hard as I could to put the blame on eight wedding showers, two big weddings, Christmas, New Year's, and several trips to a favorite soda fountain in Florida, the Lord wouldn't let me do it. I can only bow before him—while I can still bend—and acknowledge the whole problem as sin. An open and shut case of lack of self-discipline.

You know, I didn't have any trouble giving up swearing or telling dirty stories, or any of the other shackles that had me bound to this world. But take away my over-dose of chocolate and my delectables, and I sit around and pout just like some spoiled child!

I even went so far as to get upset with the Lord for giving me one of those "slow metabolisms" that doesn't burn up "fat" as quickly as others. It would especially hurt when I'd see some lovely young creature eating circles around me and never gaining an ounce! I felt like stamping my feet and saying, "Lord, it just isn't fair!"

And then one day, I was standing in front of the downstairs mirror trying on a "basic black" that USED to fit.

An observing off-spring said, "Hey, great, Mom. If you ever go to a masquerade, you can wear that and go as a pot-bellied stove." He has become pretty adept at ducking pillows, so I missed him.

"Listen, you birds! Venus de Milo was a bit thick through the middle, but they've sure made a big fuss over *her* down through the years!"

Same meddling off-spring, "Yeah—but didn't you ever notice? They had to cut off both arms to keep her from eating so much!"

By then we were all laughing merrily. And I had to admit they were right.

Satan had whispered some real smooth things into my ear, too. Like, "Your husband sure looks sharp. Young, good physique. He's not proud of you like you are of him."

That one hurt.

So the time had come. I could no longer hide behind, "I've had six children, you know."

The Lord was dealing with me most uncomfortably in the area of discipline. I knew well the verse that read, "To obey is better than sacrifice." And daily discipline in this area would come under obedience. Even fasting, which would come under "sacrifice," would have been much easier for me. But daily, regimented doing-without-delectables? I'd sure need the Lord.

I used to tease Gene and tell him I'd go on a diet when he could grow back his hair—but he has always had such an ingenious way for getting off the hook. He started combing his hair forward in such a manner that he managed to hide the receding forehead in a remarkable way from the whole world!

Well, discipline is only half the answer. The other half is found in Psalm 139, and throughout Psalm 119. These two chapters have much to say about the Lord's having formed us and shaped us the way we are for His own reasons and His own delight. In Psalm 119, verse 73 I read, "Thy hands have made me and fashioned me. . . ." So not only is self-discipline necessary, but self-acceptance. Even to the "slow metabolism." My "slow metabolism" makes it possible for me to sit here and write to you, and to study, and pray, and counsel with people without getting in a frenzy if all the loads of laundry didn't get done—

Love,
Char

LETTER THIRTY-FOUR

Dear Lennie,

God always comes through! Just when you need that word of encouragement, that lift—He causes it to come about.

I'd been sitting around, gritting my teeth because of my strict, regimented diet. Now don't misunderstand me—I'm not hungry. But in all honesty, I must tell you that my flesh is screaming out for something—anything—delectable! For three weeks I've tried to convince myself that a dill pickle tastes like a candy bar! And no matter how hard I try to think thin, I always wind up thinking triangle.

I decided it would be wise to get my mind busy before I started gnawing on the woodwork, so I started the book *Maria* by Maria von Trapp. Little did she realize how she would minister to me by a quote from something that "used to be said in the Catholic wedding ceremony—that sacrifice is usually irksome, but love can make it easy, and perfect love can make it a joy!"

I felt chagrined. Here God has given me the

challenge of additional discipline by giving me the kind of metabolism that doesn't burn up the "excess" as a means of learning self-denial, and I hadn't yet learned to embrace it as something valuable—but only as irksome and unpleasant. I remember a pastor's telling me once that all of Christendom had lost the art of self-denial.

And so, Betsy and I decided that we were pulling a serious boner by not praising God for this extra opportunity for self-denial and that we'd be better off to do away with the pouting.

Who's Betsy? She's another one of these lovely, lovely people God keeps dropping into my life.

It all happened in the Christian bookstore where so many interesting things happen to me.

Betsy was behind the counter, smiling her disarming smile and saying, "You don't know me, do you? I'm Betsy. We took the people from the nursing home out to the park together, remember?"

(How could I *forget!* I wondered if she recalled how I forgot to set the brake on one dear old soul's wheelchair, and she went sailing into the bumper of a truck. One of her compassionate peers said, "Aw, she's always complaining. Just put her out in the sun. She'll heal.")

Of course I remembered!

But Betsy didn't look the same. She was less glamorous . . . but more beautiful. She was quieter, more subdued. Her hair was back to its natural color; the false eye lashes were gone. No wonder I didn't recognize her.

We only had a moment to talk as she was busy, but I heard something in her voice . . . a plea for help, a need for fellowship.

So when she said, "Tomorrow is my day off. May I come over?" I assured her that would be fine, and began to pray about our visit.

She'd said something that had disturbed me greatly. It seems that the reason I hadn't seen Betsy around Zion Chapel lately was because she had gotten into this web Satan so often weaves, better known as the "I can do it myself—just me and Jesus" web.

It seems that she didn't "feel" a part of the fellowship so "she-and-the-Lord" would be sufficient for her. Betsy is divorced, so she didn't have the protection or covering of her husband. That made it a bit easier for her to go off on her own tangent.

It seems she got mixed up with some "straying" charismatics that were being terribly deceived by Satan. As you might have guessed, they were women. Two women who refused to submit to their own pastor, and decided they would start their own "church." Betsy was too young in the Lord to know the dangers of not being submitted to a body of believers, and too young to realize that because Eve was deceived, you need to be very leery of other unsubmitted women, who have a natural bent for going "off on a tangent."

She had suffered at the hands of these women, trying to get out of the web they'd gotten her in.

And I was upset because I know experiences like this are the very thing that leaves a bad taste in peoples' mouths when you mention "charismatic." They only remember the kooks. (Only those "off on a tangent.") They never investigate the "sane" ones! And I've discovered that charismatics off on tangents can be real nuisances and stumbling blocks. Satan sees to that!

Betsy had been all messed up in drugs at one time. As she sat there telling me her story, I couldn't help but think of how lovely she was now—that the lessons she'd learned had been hard ones, but most worthwhile, for without suffering there can be no glory—and Betsy had suffered. She'd tried to be all that her husband wanted her to be—glamorous, sexy, and basically phony, to put it her way. And when she became all these things, it wasn't what he wanted, either. And so Betsy and her little daughter tackled this big world by themselves. It was then that Betsy's "search" began. For all the kids tell me that drugs is a part of the search, that anyone who takes drugs *is* searching. . . .

She flipped out on acid, and the scare was enough to drive her right into Jesus. She went on to receive the baptism of the Holy Spirit. But from there she became a wanderer and tried to make it on her own—to "avoid the hurts I was receiving from other Christians." (This was even *before* the bad experience with the two deceived women.)

I said, "Betsy, what were some of the hurts?"

She said, "Like I never felt a part of the fellowship, and it was like you had to stand up and say something if you wanted to be noticed. And when I left, no one tried to get me to come back, like they never even noticed I was there."

Betsy had formerly been a model. Her life was built on vanity. From her own lips I heard her say that she at one time had spent at least three hours a day before a mirror, but that she was so happy to be free of all that. But when we were talking about not being noticed in the fellowship, she said, "Is it so wrong to want to be noticed—to want attention? Isn't it human and natural?"

I waited for a moment before I answered. If I spoke out the things I was feeling, and had so often felt, would they be received in the right spirit? I knew that recognition and acceptance were important to all of us, but somehow I felt Betsy's problem went deeper than simple recognition. I decided to take the plunge.

"Betsy, our problem as a whole is our "self." Our need to be pampered—to be noticed. Not just for you, Betsy, but for all of us. But somehow I think God is doing a new thing. Let me explain."

I cupped my hands together on the table.

"Betsy, here is the fellowship—the meeting place where God meets his people corporately, and blesses them with His presence. There should be —and really I think there is—such a magnetism, such a blessing available, that we should be *irresist-*

180

ibly drawn *to* the fellowship . . . to the meetings there because of *His* presence.

"You see, we have no calling program like the institutional church has. Now, the calling program is very effective. It adds numbers. But God's way is to *woo* people back in, Himself. I dare say He permitted you to sit out there in the cold without any attention because He knew that was the one thing you needed to "die to" more than anything else!

"Be honest, Betsy. If we had come after you, would we not have been catering to your self-pity —your need for attention? But our meeting in the bookstore was not by chance. God set it up. He wanted you to hear these things."

Her face lit up. She was receiving all this well.

I went on to say, "More and more I'm realizing this whole business of dying to self is what it's all about. God wants us to die out to some very human desires so that His life of power can shine through —do you see what I mean, Betsy?"

Her eyes were shining. The idea had caught on. We then turned to I Peter 11 where Paul talks about suffering. And in my Amplified Bible, it says that "suffering is inseparable from our vocation."

I said, "Betsy, those so-called hurts were the very chisels God wanted to use to mold you into the image of His Son. They were to teach you how to be forbearing and forgiving—to enable you to love the 'unlovely.' "

181

She said, "Wow. That's heavy." She underlined the verse and other verses that brought out the meaning more clearly.

". . . and Betsy, nowhere in the Bible are we commanded to 'feel' loved. We are commanded to *give* love, *expecting nothing in return*. This is a lesson I had to learn the hard way, because I've spent so much of my life giving love with one hand, while extending the other to see what the other person would give in return."

Lennie, this whole business of being a Christian is meant to be more than a social club. Its whole aim is one of being conformed into the image of His Son. And conforming means changing. And changing means doing some things differently than we did before. And it means having our minds renewed, our thinking processes reversed and rearranged. But the goal is fantastic— that we might be like Him. That we might have the "mind of Christ" with all these things being very obtainable—not impossible, as some would have you to think!

Like I said—it's exciting!

More later,
Char

LETTER THIRTY-FIVE

Dear Lennie,

I really shouldn't take this time, but I was just tip-toeing by the typewriter, trying not to look at it—when "zingo" there I was—I mean here I am, stealing a bit of ironing time to get this line off to you.

Have I got ironing? Lennie, my ironing is *so* big—I've considered giving it all to the Goodwill so I could buy it back after they've mended and ironed it!

Truly, we've become a half-way house. Washing's half done, ironing's half done—but most of all, many come here because they are only "half way" to Jesus. (You should see these dear souls wending their way through the piles of laundry to get to the coffee pot, that's—you guessed it! Half-empty!)

Some of these dear souls are "hippies." I don't know what the neighbors think about all the "long hairs" they've seen dropping by—nor is it important. But everytime I holler out the door and say "Mark! Time to cut the 'grass' again," I'm always wondering if I should have yelled "lawn," and why is that squad car circling our block?

Once, several months ago, four of these individualists came to our door. They really hadn't come for counseling. They'd just dropped by to borrow Don's drum set—seems they used to go to school with him. (When I peeked into the almost hidden eyes behind all that hair I thought they looked somewhat familiar.)

They happened to come in and catch me trying to tune up my guitar. (And I'm happy to say they controlled their laughter much better than you would have under the same circumstances.) One of them, being a guitarist, offered to tune it for me while asking, "How'd you ever happen to take up the guitar?" (I'm sure they thought bandage rolling would have been more in line with my age as forty to them would be over the hill.)

I commented, "If I'm going to be taken for a Jesus Freak, I might as well look like one. And fellas, don't laugh—because my fingers are so sore from trying to conquer this thing, I believe they'd glow in the dark," as I limply held up my tender left paw.

Little did I realize that the remark about being a Jesus Freak would be used of God to open a door. I had no idea their hearts were so hungry—although they have since told me that any kid on drugs is on drugs simply for that reason—that he is hungry and is searching. Isn't it strange how we

184

all insist on trying Satan's counterfeits before we will settle for the real thing?

Well, after two or three "rap" sessions with Gene and me, three of the four accepted Christ, and two asked for the baptism in the Holy Spirit. At first they didn't latch onto the things of God. They came to meetings only spasmodically. They seemed to lack interest. But Gene and I refused to be anything but positive in our confession and praying because we believed that Jesus was the author of their new-found faith, and, according to His Word, He would also be the finisher of it, and we would hold Him to that.

I'm very happy to say that after some real rough starts—and jolts—and spurts—two of these have really taken hold of the things of God, and really mean business with the Lord.

Their hair isn't long and ragged anymore. It's clean and short and a testimony to the wisdom of allowing external things to take care of themselves, as no one ever told them to get their hair cut. They just simply wanted to and felt "led" to do it.

Interestingly enough, the third young man who accepted Christ still has the long unkempt hair, doesn't come to the meetings, nor is he willing to submit to a body of believers. Guess he thinks he can do his own thing. Once when someone had unwisely made a remark about his hair, he retorted "I have to have my hair like this so I can identify with the kids I want to reach. . . ."

To which my husband quietly remarked "Not by might, nor by power, *nor by your long hair,* but by MY spirit, saith the Lord. . . ."

The fourth young man is still searching . . . and we are still praying.

Oh, Lennie—gotta run. 'Nother crisis. Jamie just took all the rubber tips off his arrows, and now he's trying to sharpen them in the pencil sharpener!

Love,
Char

LETTER THIRTY-SIX

Dear Lennie,

God keeps sending these young, attractive mothers my way. At times I'm tempted to plead, "Lord, How 'bout a nice, plump, plain one . . . someone I can identify with, Lord?" And the more I thought about pleading this, the more attractive the young mothers were!

Yet, I'm always amazed at the inferiorities even these most attractive ones have. Once one of these lovely creatures said, "Why do I feel like I never look nice? I don't see how my husband could ever love me—I feel so unattractive."

And I sat there being almost envious of her peaches-and-cream complexion, her tiny waistline and her graceful hands. I pulled my tummy in, sat on both hands, and hoped she'd notice the twinkle *in* my eyes instead of the wrinkles *surrounding* them.

I assured her that I knew all about feelings of inferiority and how they can paralyze you at times. But I also told her that I'd learned years ago that it isn't how you LOOK that affects people so much, but whether or not they feel comfortable in your presence.

I shared with her that my feelings of inferiority have dimished as I have grown in the Lord, because of the assurance that I am totally acceptable to Him.

But there are still times when I suffer. Like the time I'd stopped in at a local drive-in to pick up some quick sandwiches. We'd been painting in the kitchen, and I was a bit dissheveled, to say the least. Well, in she breezed, fresh from a crisp wrapper—dear Caryl.

Caryl has always meant a lot to me, because when we were both about fourteen, we were sitting in church together. The pastor had just given an invitation for those who would like to accept Christ. Now, I hate to admit this, but I think we'd both been writing notes to each other for the whole length of the sermon. She whispered "Hey, would you like to go up front and accept Christ as your Savior? I'll walk up there with you. . . ."

"You mean in front of all these PEOPLE? Not me!"

"Oh, come on . . . I did . . . you'll feel real good after your knees quit shaking."

And in that moment, somewhere between the eleventh pew and the front of that church that seemed a mile away, new life was sparked within me. I became born again!

And here she was again! But, oh, why did I have to look like this! And why did she have to look like *that!* Beautifully coiffed, manicured, and wrinkle free—clothes *and* complexion.

The moment she said, "Charlene, so good to see you," I limply said, "Yes, good to see you too, Caryl." And sheer panic gripped me because I felt that if I were to glance down, I'd find my coat was buttoned wrong. I even imagined I could feel the hair growing on my legs! But the panic lasted for only a moment, because this was Caryl! We'd shared too many laughs, too many hurts to allow my creepy inferiorities to tie me up in knots at just this time—so Christ was victor as we shared things the Lord had been doing for us, and as we talked we both laughed uproariously when I discovered that Caryl HAS to look like she stepped fresh from a wrapper, because her own inferiorities are so unbearable for her, this is the only way she can live with them! We decided that inferiorities are just one of the tasteless things left in each human being from Adam's fall that have to be endured and overcome by those who are determined to be overcomers.

If we could just keep the image before us that we see in the mirror. If we have safely bordered on this side of vanity, I mean. Hair brushed neatly, powdered nose, collar lying flat, no slip showing. But my problem is that every time I get to whereever I'm going, I forget about what I saw in the mirror. I only remember that as I was sailing hurriedly out the door, I had to intercept one Oreo-cookie kiss, one Mom-I-just-caught-a-big-carp hug that had a fishy aroma to it. And once outside the door, the adoring sheep dog leaped up on me to say good-bye, and then I remembered the trailing thread of bubble gum that went from the third step of the porch clear to the accelerator.

Well, it will do us all good to consider that it isn't whether or not we are so perfectly groomed, but whether or not people are "comfortable" with us. That should be our goal. And if we will just learn that valuable lesson of Phillippians 2:4—of looking "on the things" (or interests) of others instead of our "own thing," then others WILL be comfortable in our presence.

Love,
Char

LETTER THIRTY-SEVEN

Dear Lennie,

I feel like a kitten with a fuzzball of experience caught in my throat. I'm quite certain the Lord wants me to spit it all out right about here, but it keeps sticking.

Maybe because it was such a humbling experience.

I mean, I'm really not accustomed to people getting up and walking out while I'm talking!

But I'm getting ahead of my story . . .

It all happened just a few days ago. I'd been invited to share with about ten ladies from a denominational church. (If Pat Boone knew which denomination, he'd turn spiritual cartwheels for a week!) When I agreed to come, I'd specifically asked that either the pastor or an elder be present to judge whether what I shared lined up with the Word of God or not. I had also told the pastor I wouldn't share anything that couldn't be backed up BY the Word of God.

As it turned out, neither the pastor or the elder could be present. I had to acknowledge the Lord in

191

this, and I felt I had done the right thing scripturally in asking them to meet with us.

We met at Vicki's house.

Now, you have to know Vicki to appreciate her. She is bold, new-in-the-Lord, and feels no need for beating around a bush—if that bush happens to be a burning one. She knew where the area of need was, so in very typical Vicki style, she blurted, "Now, give 'em all that good stuff you gave me about being in submission to your husband, and obedience, and things like that. . . ."

I felt as though I'd been shoved into the center of an arena—with a pitch fork. I faced those questioning eyes and secretly wondered who were my enemies and who were my friends. Faithful Judy (remember, Lennie? the "Judy" who went to Florida with us) was by my side praying, praise God.

I took a good firm stand upon the Word of God, and started in with, "Uh, well—I think—I'm wondering if— Let's turn to I Peter 3—" as I became vaguely conscious that I could be out there on that most uncomfortable limb, again.

I can best describe the encounter by saying it was a spiritual battle like I hadn't encountered for some time. This was one of my reasons for wanting a man present. I believe personally that Satan can not have an upper hand when men are present, but that he can have a heyday in their absence, because of Eve's unfortunate episode in the garden, and because of the cold fact that women are more easily deceived than men. I think they should even be present when there is a small gathering, if that gathering is for the purpose of sharing the things of God.

I was touching on my personal belief that the Word of God says exactly what it means when it asks wives to be subject to their husbands in *EVERY*thing as it says in Ephesians 5:24. (Amplified Bible. As you can tell, I use it constantly.)

I was expounding to my heart's content about this piece of scripture, when I noticed a lovely young mother named Tina, crying as though her heart would break.

She interrupted me by saying, "You *can't* know —you can't understand—how could you know! My husband doesn't want me to go to church— he says he doesn't want me 'brainwashing' his son with all this Jesus talk! Now don't tell me you expect me to submit to THAT!"

I said, "Tina, I can only tell you that the Word of God says EVERYTHING, but there are other references we need to look at . . ."

And as I was busily hunting for the second chapter of I Peter where God speaks of "suffering . . ." as being a "part of our vocation," and where a bit further on He speaks about Christ's "trusting Himself and everything to Him Who judges fairly" —SHE LEFT!

I didn't know whether I should follow her, or

just what I should do. Judy hopped up and went to convince her that she should stay, but Tina was determined to leave.

I felt so torn—how could I tell her that she could trust her little boy into the hands of God because the area of "trust" is the very area God was working on? I'd failed her, somehow, or she wouldn't have run off like that. And I knew it wouldn't do any good to call on her. I had the feeling she would just as soon stay as far from me as she could.

I had to face the fact, reluctantly, that I'd never be able to explain what I still had to say to her— that the power of God would probably not flow into the situation until she relinquished it all into His hands. Had I made it clear to her that God loved her rebellious husband more than she ever could? That He cared for his soul, and her little boy's? Lennie, she was gone . . .

I ministered somewhat feebly to the other women because my heart was so much upon Tina. I had to wrestle with their "opinions" and "ideas" they had developed down through the years. Well, in some ways it was a pretty bad scene. But I feel the Holy Spirit will continue to deal with Tina, because she later told her pastor that she had to leave because everything that was being said seemed to "point right to me and I couldn't take it."

But I feel confident that everything I said was based upon the Word of God. If His Spirit spoke to their spirits that what I was saying was true— then only good can come from that meeting.

It was the feeling of helplessness I had trouble coping with. The feeling that maybe I hadn't spoken in love—had I been too abrupt? I had to hand it all to the Lord and ask Him to remedy whatever had been wrong on my part and to deal with her as tenderly (or as severely) as was necessary to get the job "done."

Well, I've spit out my fuzzball. Guess this kitten on the keys had better get busy elsewhere.

Love,
Char

LETTER THIRTY-EIGHT

Dear Lennie,

Just time for a quick line to you before I run downtown. We had a home meeting here last night. Again, we felt the sweet presence of the Lord.

But the tenderest scene happened after the meeting.

A young married man in the fellowship had been trying for some time to catch Gene alone. We figured he just wanted some private counseling.

So, last night Gene and—let's call him Jack—went into the living room as his young wife and I cleaned up the kitchen.

About twenty minutes later they came out. I had to blink my eyes. For a moment I thought they might have been on the mount with Moses—or present at the transfiguration, or something! Their faces were absolutely radiant! Gene could only speak softly and about all he could say when he did speak was, "Praise the Lord—thank you, Jesus—Jesus, I love You."

I ushered the young couple to the door, said

goodnight to them, then went to talk with my dazed husband.

"Honey, you obviously got blessed—anything I can share in?"

Gene said quietly "He needed to confess something to me. . . ." He said it so quietly, I didn't fully understand.

"Did Jack have a bad attitude toward you? Was that the problem?"

"Char—remember the break-in at the store a year or so ago?"

"Yes, but . . . you don't mean?

"Yes. That boy came to me and confessed it, knowing full well I could have him prosecuted. He wants to make full restitution. He says he thinks he knows where some of the merchandise is. If he can't get it back from the 'others' involved, he said he would pay for it."

Of course I was thrilled, but poor Jack . . . did he have any idea how long it would take him to pay back what had been taken? He and his "friends" had taken some pretty expensive merchandise!

But Gene interrupted my thoughts with "Char —don't you see the best part of all? God's willingness to see that our specific prayers get answers— it's fantastic! Do you realize that when he knelt with us here in our family room to accept Christ a few months ago, he knew then that he had stolen from us! He probably needed to establish a better relationship with the Lord before he could bring himself to confess it—and Char," he put his arm around me, "do you remember how we prayed after the break-in? How we asked God to convict the consciences of those who broke in? Wow! There seems to be no end to God's surprises!"

Lennie, Jack could have found Christ at anyone's house, but God allowed it to happen here, so we could know our "specific" prayers were answered. Hallelujah!

Love,
Char

LETTER THIRTY-NINE

Dear Lennie,

I've just been reading a book by Andrew Murray, *The Holiest of All*. He uses Scripture to prove that just one tiny drop of the Savior's precious blood is enough to cleanse us for all time and eternity.

I thought, "How can that be?" I saw myself down through the years and all the rebellion I had against Him. I saw all the bad things I'd done. And then I saw the *good* things I'd done, and the credit *I'd* taken for having done them. How could one tiny drop cover up so much sin in just one life, let alone all the millions that have put their faith in that precious blood? . . . "It's almost too much to comprehend, Lord," I whispered.

And then, ever so gently the Holy Spirit made me to think about the two thousand years that have passed since He gave Himself for us . . . and suddenly, I realized . . . that my life was so small . . . my possible 70 or 80 years (more or less, depending on His plan) were so insignificant in comparison to all those years . . . that any impact I might have on this crazy mixed-up world would need a microscope to be even noticed!

Suddenly, I was able to crawl happily beneath that one tiny drop, and dip and bathe and rejoice in it forevermore. Even now, when I come to Him in prayer, I get a mental picture of the immensity of that one drop—what it accomplished for all time —and my smallness in comparison to it.

Truly, that one drop is sufficient! It's all I need! It cleanses me completely and will never fail me! Oh, Hallelujah!

Love,
Char

LETTER FORTY

Dear Lennie,

Honestly, sometimes I feel like I'm leading two lives. The one is all cluttered up with dentist appointments, things to be dropped off, places I'm expected to be and responsibilities that can't be ignored. The other is the meaningful one in the Spirit—that is hid with Christ in God. I perform these superficial duties because they are expected of me, but the other just flows on ever so quietly, giving root and meaning to the "things" expected of me.

Lennie, something terrible has happened. Maybe that's why I don't sound quite as cheerful . . . I'm experiencing a taste of mourning.

Just a few days ago, I looked into the face of a young mother of about thirty-seven.

She was lying in a casket, in a heavily rose-scented funeral parlor. She had taken her own life. I can't tell you what pulsated through me when I stood before that casket. I think it was pure hatred for Satan and all his deceptive ways.

I asked her husband, "Why, Sam?"

He could only look at me pitifully and say, "I don't know, Char. She wanted something . . . she couldn't tell me what it was . . . she couldn't put it into words."

How my heart ached! For the unnameable longings of the heart can only be satisfied in Christ! Oh, why was there no one to tell her? Why hadn't our paths crossed through the years? Why aren't there more with a working knowledge of Christ to go to these desperate souls? Is it because we haven't prayed to the Lord of the harvest and asked Him to thrust them out? Why do we always think of that prayer in terms of the heathen in Africa?

I'll write more later, when my heart is not so heavy.

Char

LETTER FORTY-ONE

Dear Lennie,

Grab yourself a quick cup of coffee and slip into something comfortable—like that old chair Les always loved so much. I've got something I want to share with you.

I need to give you some of the details because it will help you to understand Proverbs 16:33b a bit more. In the Amplified Bible it says ". . . even the events that seem (accidental) are really ordered by Him."

It happened like this.

Laurie and I were stuck with each other for company as Gene was out of town and the boys were with another family for the day, so we thought we'd be really genteel and go out for Sunday dinner.

I said, "Steak house?"

She said "Mom—you can't kid me. You want some of that chocolate pie they serve there. Let's do you a favor and go to that new cafeteria. They don't have home-baked pies there."

I sighed, wondering how I could be so fortunate to have so many "policemen" watching out for my good.

And so, we waited in a line that seemed endless, but it was kind of fun as I seldom have Laurie all to myself anymore. She is fast getting into that stage of teen-age development that seems to warrant only a vague look when her name is called out. I'd begun to think maybe I should wear a name tag around the house just to jar her memory occasionally. Having gone through this era a number of times before, it didn't concern me too much . . . especially when I knew I'd be a real smash hit as a babysitter when the grandchildren started coming along. So an opportunity to renew our relationship was most welcome.

Just as we were about to look for a place to sit, someone peeked through the lattice-work and said, "ps-s-s-st—two available seats here if you like good company."

I shrieked as quietly as one can shriek in a cafeteria without drawing too much attention.

Marge and Ellen! I hadn't seen either of them for a couple of months, and I knew they'd been going through some rough waters, both of them. I was so happy to see them!

Marge and Ellen had been thrown into each other's company by a series of strange—seemingly accidental—circumstances. Only a few months before, Marge's husband had left her after twenty-seven years of marriage. Ellen's husband was still "living" at her address, but was carrying on a flagrant affair with another woman. In their intense hurt and despair, Marge and Ellen had been crying out to the Lord for someone to share with—someone who would understand, and He led them to one another.

Marge and Ellen both loved the Lord. They were both struggling with the suffering that comes from choosing obedience to the Word of God over and above the world's way that says, "Go ahead and do your own thing; you've had a dirty deal; now have a fling; this is your chance. Why don't you get even?"

God had brought them together so that when one fell into despair, the other would be there to encourage and strengthen. And here we all were, brought together by the Lord, and for His own reasons.

You see, I'd been going through a bad time myself. I'd been focusing too much upon my circumstances again, and refusing to see the hand of God *in* them. I'd pushed aside the element of trust and had gotten back into some of my old habits of murmuring and complaining.

This was a time of real testing for me. I knew that I had to take all my circumstances as from the Lord—especially those circumstances that came through my husband's decisions, as he is the one directly over me in authority. For the most part, I had been able to accept this. But there are times when the battle has to be fought over again—perhaps time and time again until the ground is *really* "secure." But interestingly enough, my battles with loneliness and separations helped me to understand at least something of what they were enduring.

As we sat there sharing over our meals, that blessed "body ministry" began that means so much. There is one thing I have to say about charismatics. Once everyone is situated comfortably, they start talking about Jesus!

As they began to share about some of the lessons they'd learned by being obedient to the Word, I was strengthened and encouraged. (And how I praise God that my separations from Gene are for such short periods—only a week or two at a time.) Then, as I shared a revelation I'd had from the Lord, I had the joy of watching as it spoke peace to their own troubled hearts.

I told them how bad things had been for me a week or so before this time. I told them that Satan was throwing the same old lines at me that he used to throw—only this time I recognized them for what they were—LIES!

There had been times when I felt as though I were being squeezed in on both sides by two thieves. On the one side, a thief of "yesterday" would say, "If only he hadn't started a second business—if only things hadn't worked out this way." And while I was still feeling the pinch on the one side, the other thief would start in—the thief of the "unknown tomorrows." He'd say, "Look down through the on-coming years—just a lot more of

206

the same—separations and goodbyes—makes you miserable, doesn't it?"

I knew I'd been spending far too much time listening to these two thieves. I decided I'd sinned against God by listening to them at all, so I went to Him for help. And, being very human, I spewed out a whole string of "facts" that were dripping with self-pity, before Him. But I got the impression that, as I prayed in this manner, He was just standing there with His arms folded—waiting. Just waiting.

He said so gently, "I know all of that. When are you going to do the thing most needful—when are you going to use the weapon I've placed in your hand? When are you going to praise Me?"

He caught me right in the middle of a sob. I realized I'd been going about it all wrong! Suddenly, the goodness of the Lord came to me. The realization that He *did* order my circumstances to meet certain needs in my life—that only those things which were the very best for me would He *ever* allow to come my way. Romans 8:28—all things working together for good—how could I rebel against such goodness? My heart lifted with praise to Him—and as I praised Him and asked forgiveness for murmuring and complaining, something wonderful happened on the inside of me. My circumstances were not changed—but my *acceptance* of the circumstances had altered! Joy began to flood my soul! By praising Him I was saying "Jesus —You know what is best for me," and with that, the element of trust was restored. But another wonderful thing happened. Those two thieves receded into the shadows, because Someone stood between them! A victorious Someone Who looked at me and said, "*Today* shalt thou be with me in paradise!"

And I knew immediately what He meant!

He was saying that we only have to live one day at a time, but that He had provided a way whereby that day could be lived *in the heavenlies!* Each day was to be a heaven on earth if we would only accept with joy the trial, the tribulation, the separation—whatever He sends our way to prove our faith and His faithfulness. That each difficulty could be either a stepping stone to maturity or a stumbling block to faith. As I prayed, my will once again got in line with His Will, and I experienced even *more* joy flooding into my heart.

Well, we had us a praise and prayer meeting right there in that cafeteria! And just before we left one another Marge said "Char—tell me one thing. Were you and Laurie thinking about going to a different place before you came here?"

I said "Yes! My mouth was watering for a piece of that pie at the steak house. . . ."

She said "I thought so. We were all led here, to share together. Isn't the Lord wonderful?"

And Lennie . . . y'know . . . He really IS!

Love—
Char

208

LETTER FORTY-TWO

Dear Lennie,

Since you remember me from the "if-you-really-love-the-Lord-you-will-be-in-church-every-time-the-doors-are-open" days, this may shock you a bit. Because it all happened on a Sunday night—and we weren't even in church. (We've discovered that two services on Sunday can be exhausting, so we don't always go. Sometimes we just keep it open for our family, or for visiting others as a family.)

On this particular Sunday night we'd gone to visit friends. Friends in the truest sense, because they accept us the way we are—"fanatically" in love with Jesus. And we accept them the way they are —not quite interested enough yet to commit their lives to Him—but interested enough to want to know what things have been going on in our lives concerning Him.

As we were rounding up the kids to head for home around 10 o'clock, my friend's younger daughter came to us and said, "Mom? why is Debbie in on my bed crying?" (Debbie is my friend's married daughter who'd come to visit them for a

209

few weeks while her husband was doing some as-signed duty.)

My friend motioned for me to come with her. I could tell by her look that she felt I could help. I was already busily praying in the Spirit, thinking that our being there was no accident. And she cer-tainly was crying . . . bitter, body-wracking sobs that came from the depths of her misery.

I knew some of the details of Debbie's life. And because her problems are so symptomatic of young marrieds all over the world, I think I should share some of the details with you.

You see, Debbie had "had" to get married. She was—and still is—a brilliant girl with great po-tential. She made her way through college on scholarships because of her brilliance. And then she met a brilliant boy. They had everything going for them—even the love that they felt for one another. But this same heady, strong, and over-powering love plunged them deeply into a situation beyond their control because they had no restraints from the fear of God, or any knowledge of the moral code God had built into them. On college campuses all over, "free love" is not looked down upon—and so at the time, they couldn't (or wouldn't) look upon this act that is legal and right within the bonds of marriage as an act of sin *outside* of mar-riage.

How I wish our young people could be taught the value of self-discipline—the art of "waiting" instead of, "I want what I want and I want it right now."

Well, this gives you some background for what happened next.

There she was, a promising young woman whose life was shattered—or so she thought—at her feet. I'd noticed during the evening that her little boy, although adorable, was also very demanding. He seemed to be somehow insecure in her love, and was unusually cantankerous. Many of her actions toward him seemed to be mingled with utter devotion and stifled impatience.

As she lay on the bed, the cry from her heart went something like this:

"I'm a prisoner to that child, Mom! I can't get away—he cries for me every minute I'm gone—and with Bob gone all the time, there's no one to help. Mom, there just *has* to be more to living than *this!* And I feel so guilty—so ashamed about the way we got married. I always feel as though people are pointing a finger at me. Especially girls I know who have done the same, only worse—I mean with more than one guy! Why do I feel so guilty now that it's so far in the past? It isn't like we weren't married! This guilt has all but ruined our sex life. . . ."

And the frustrated young wife buried her red eyes into the pillow.

My friend, being all mother, began to console her by saying, "Honey, you don't need to feel guilty

—lots of others have done the same thing—*you're* not so bad."

And that's when the Holy Spirit began to move in. I so admire His tact—His timing. Because if I hadn't learned to follow His leading, I'd have barged in there ahead of schedule and spent the rest of the time picking up the pieces. I've learned that He will make an individual whole in His own tender way—not our jarring shattering way—the way of the "flesh."

I am so grateful to the Lord for having brought a book across my path just a few days previous to this encounter. The name of the book is *Competant to Counsel* by Jay Adams. In this book he brought out the importance of recognizing people's guilt as needing to be taken seriously, and that to minimize that guilt is the same as saying, "I don't take you seriously." The book also proves by using the many scriptures that refer to the command to exhort, rebuke, and admonish one another (in love), that we, the Christians, are better equipped to deal with the needs of the human heart than the most learned psychologists and psychiatrists! (Many of them don't even know Christ.)

At any rate, the Holy Spirit prompted me to put this theory to work, and "work" it does. When I suggested that she face this thing, this "guilt," and lay it squarely before the Lord because He considered the act as sinful outside of marriage in spite of anything she may have picked up in college to the contrary, that He had built into us a moral code that no "new morality" could undo.

I helped her to see that before God what she had done *was* sin—but that God still loved her and had made a way for her sin to be covered and forgiven. He would remove the sense of guilt if she would just accept the provision for the removal of sin He had provided in His Son Jesus.

There was another obstacle in her way—her college education. She said, "It's all going to waste! I'm not doing a thing with that education."

About here, America could use a good verbal spanking. We wonder what's wrong with our youth, when we are turning out mothers that have never been trained to *be* mothers. The whole thrust of our educational system is "the key to success lies in knowledge—get an education, and unhappiness will be eliminated! Educate the heathen and they will have happiness! Go for that degree! Never mind preparing for motherhood—you can wedge that in somewhere, sometime."

And we mothers are at fault, too. Instead of putting baby dolls that wet into our daughters' arms, we run out and buy dress-up teenage dolls with emphasis on style, fashion, dating and party-going. I discovered that mothers in Europe are trained and taught and exhorted to *long* to be mothers, and mothers in the truest sense as a vocation, as a dream—not just something alongside of a job, an education—something you become when you don't have a chance to become something else.

Well, God had a blessing in store for our Debbie,

because she was open and sincere in her confession. She honestly didn't want to be the way she was, but she didn't know where to turn. Praise God, she turned the right way—to Him. She asked Christ to come into her heart that night, and was relieved of that load of guilt. She found peace with God, and began to think of her role as wife and mother as the highest calling she could have.

Her mother told me later that the obvious change in Debbie had caused *her* to do some serious thinking, too. I can't help but feel that a "new birth" experience is just around the corner for her as well.

As I've typed all this out to you, I am reminded of another young woman I knew who had married under these same "conditions." She carried a great burden around inside of her because she always wondered, "Did my husband marry me because he loved me—or because he 'had' to." But someone came along with a great deal of sense and told her that "it doesn't seem all that important whether he loved you or not when you were married. The important question is—does he love you NOW!"

That bit of wisdom cleared the issue up for her for all time, as he was a devoted husband, and I pass it on to you so that others might be helped by it.

More later—
Char

214

LETTER FORTY-THREE

Dear Lennie,

I'll sure be glad when the Lord finally has me perfected to the place that He can use fine sandpaper instead of a chiseling tool!

I've come to value the body ministry more each day, as He uses them to make me conformed to the image of Christ. Every now and then I look down at my feet and see how many chips have fallen, and I say, "Whew! I'm glad that's over!"

Since I've signed the contract for the book, a few have said, "Aren't you afraid of becoming proud?"

I say, "No. I'm afraid of God. Besides, He has placed me in just the right body of believers to eliminate just such a possibility—and I praise Him for it! I love my brothers and sisters in Christ more deeply every day, and thank God for giving them to me as instruments of His grace to mold me into His image."

Several years ago (back in those nerve-wracking days when I thought I had to knock myself out by being the comedienne of the day in order for people to love me) I was "entertaining" a few saints who were gracious enough to laugh in all the right places. Our pastor at that time kind of shook his head, as though he might be wondering why God put me in his particular fold.

I glanced his way and said "Pastor, you might as well adjust to me now, because my Bible says we'll be spending all of Eternity together."

He rolled his eyes dramatically and glanced heavenward and said, "Ah, yes—I know. But praise the Lord, we'll all be changed!"

Well, praise the Lord, we don't have to wait until He comes back to be changed! And I think that's good news for all of us who have to put up with one another the way we are, in order for Him to work long-suffering in us. Because I'm finding out that He sends some pretty unlovable people our way.

I remember praising the Lord once in a meeting, eyes closed and arms reaching to heaven—oh, I felt so holy. I heard someone come in and sit beside me. I peeked, and everything inside of me said, "Ugh." I said, "Oh, *no*—you don't really expect me to love *that*, do you Lord?"

"Of course. I died for him, just like I died for you. Now get on with it."

I avoided this particular person like the plague— mostly because he looked like he could infect me WITH one, when out of a clear blue, sky-high testimony meeting, we found ourselves trapped in a situation where we'd have to converse.

Oh, Lennie. I felt so small. I discovered that

beneath the exterior of that person was a man who loved Jesus passionately, with a zeal that made me look like warmed-up death. And he was extremely delightful! Humor that warmed your heart and deep compassion for the underdog.

How happy I am that the Lord taught me not to look on the outside appearance, but on the heart. And this isn't always so easy to do, since most people have ordered their lives in such a way that you can't even catch a glimpse of their heart. But not so with charismatics! It's their very hunger for heart-to-heart rapport that got them into this "movement" anyhow.

Now how did all this happen? I was going to tell you about my operation!

Love,
Char

LETTER FORTY-FOUR

Dear Lennie,

I know the Lord has a sense of humor because He made monkeys—and me. I also know He has an understanding heart because He put up with me and all my idiosyncrasies so patiently during the "wilderness" years.

Like, when once upon a swimming pool I declared, "Lord, we're going to build one. Now bless it to our bodies' use, O Lord."

We made the decision to build the pool because . . . well, because I always used to get my own way, I guess.

This all happened several sticky summers ago, before the encounter with the Holy Spirit.

I overheard my kids making plans that would eventually bring about the nervous breakdown I had been so carefully avoiding.

As I listened, I discovered all of their plans included water. They painted glowing pictures of sandy beaches, cozy cabins and faraway places.

But I came up with some mental artistry of my own.

I saw this weary mother trudging through blistering sand, toting ice chests, life vests, baskets, flippers, goggles, lotions, notions, beachballs, and inflating a couple of rubber duckies all the while. Their idea of an action-packed summer was more than my own lazy inclinations cared to cope with. I knew I had to redirect their enthusiasm or that breakdown might be my only out!

And so, the idea of a swimming pool began to ply its way up through my subconscious. Its little tendrils gently choked out, "can we afford it?" and were working their way up through, "what will the neighbors think?" when I presented it to my unsuspecting husband. And just as quickly, it entwined its way around his unsuspecting ulcer. He finally agreed that a swimming pool would be a perfect solution to our summer dilemma, after just the right amount of tearful persuasion.

For we really did have a summer dilemma, because we'd found out in a hurry that the only place you could go with six kids and be *really* welcome was to Sunday School! And we *did* love them very much. Individually, that is. Collectively and in a small area like a car, we couldn't *stand* them! So-o-o-o it was settled. We would do our vacationing and entertaining in our own backyard.

The kids were elated! They even offered to help pay for the pool. They sold their pet turtles, favorite marbles and one little "con artist" (who was only about three at the time) even sold the white rocks out of our driveway. My neighbor said her sales pitch included something about her Mommy and Daddy needing lots and lots of money. But it hadn't taken long for the word to leak out that the profits were to go for a swimming pool, and sales were phenomenal before she got grounded. (We were now seeing weeds where white rock used to be.)

So, the day finally came when we met with the pool contractor. We were a bit hesitant at first. But he made it sound so simple. He assured us that there was "very little upkeep" and also convinced us that everyone with six kids was getting a pool nowadays. I kind of got a queasy feeling in my stomach as Gene signed on the first line as I wasn't sure we could even afford such a luxury. But then again, I didn't see how they could ever repossess a cement swimming pool, so I signed on the bottom line and decided to settle back and enjoy the whole misadventure.

They began digging the pool on my birthday. I think it was a coincidence, but Gene decided to take advantage of the coincidence by pointing to the pool with pride and exclaiming, "Yep! Got it for Char's birthday!" He has said it on every birthday since. And Christmas. And anniversary. He said it was the gift to end all gifts—and it did!

The day the pool was dug was akin to a national holiday. Neighbors gathered from the four corners of the block to supervise. The Hoosier humidity played well its role in our little drama. The temperature was in the unbearable half of the

220

nineties. This convinced us that the decision to build the pool had been a good one.

In the middle of the site we had chosen for our pool stood a fine young maple tree. It made us all sad to know it would have to go, but only the day before, a man from the nursery had told us a tree of its size could never withstand transplanting in the tremendous heat. And, as it looked much like any other tree, being green at the top and brown at the bottom, the sadness was soon replaced by keen interest as we watched the huge piece of earth moving equipment tear it away from its earthly security.

But we didn't realize that to the neighbors the tree had become a very *special* tree. When they found out we were not going to at least attempt a transplant they descended on us angrily. One glance, and I knew we were dealing with a lynch mob. Bert shouted, "Why, it would cost you three hundred dollars to replace a tree like that!" I'll admit that shook me a little. Thelma grabbed the hose and began to spray the tree with a fine spray and ordered, "Keep it wet! Just keep it wet! I know it will grow!"

The tender sapling, now chained to the back of the huge crane was looking a little worse for the wear.

"Lady, where d'ya want this tree? I've got a pool to dig!" thundered a voice from inside the crane. Frantically, I looked around and decided that the only logical place for such a tree would be in the front, directly by my kitchen window. I had visions of lacy shadows dancing across my greasy dishwater come next spring.

Now, I had a big front yard. Barren and bald, but big. However, it did go rather well with the sparsely pebbled driveway. I hurriedly picked out the bald spot where I thought the tree should go, then stepped aside to watch the lumbering crane come across our drive (cracking a large piece of cement to add to the now mounting list of hidden expenses) and sink its huge jaws into the sod.

And then the unexpected happened.

The crane had obviously bitten off more than it could chew, for the grinding of its gears were drowned out by a horrible grating sound. Not only had it bitten into the sod, but came up chewing on our gas line as well. The meter was torn from the inside of the house, and a sinister hiss warned that gas was quietly but powerfully being expelled over the entire neighborhood. Within minutes, gas men were swarming all over the premises, scratching their heads and muttering, "I wonder if that woman's for real!"

The tree was finally transplanted in another gaping hole, and remained there for quite some time, looking very much like any of the other things I have ever planted. Brown at the bottom, and at the top, too. There were no lacy shadows. Only cobwebs.

After ten days of frenzied construction, our pool

was ready. Now all we needed was 22,000 gallons of water.

Have you ever wondered how swimming pools are filled?

Ver-r-r-y slowly.

We didn't bathe, drink, or cook while three garden hoses and a panting pump struggled three days and nights to fill our concrete wonder.

Finally, with parched lips, one of my children ran in on the third day to rasp, "Mother, it's filled!" And sure enough, it was. It was filled to the brim . . . with ice water.

When we ~~ the pool in, my children were much smaller, and their friends likewise. As we were primarily dealing with small fry, it worked out very well to make a firm rule that you had to be within running range of your own familiar bath-room if you wanted to claim our pool for your summer home.

And then one day, my children were suddenly very big. Their friends were very big, too. Big enough for me to be willing to share my own bath-room rather than risk an argument with them. So big, they came in droves, by car, on tandems, on Hondas . . . even via horse and buggy.

You see, we had a young girl helping us who belonged to a religious denomination that didn't go in for frivolities, so they were still using a horse and buggy.

And one muggy July Sunday afternoon, there

stood a buggy in my driveway, big as life—horse and all. I couldn't recall making eyes at any of the egg men in our area that drive such a rig, and was wondering which neighbor might think I had, when I recognized my helper's laugh among some other strange voices in the pool.

I was about to pinch myself to see if all this was really happening. But it wasn't necessary, as there was proof enough in the driveway! After they left, I shoveled the proof under the rose bushes and wondered what could possibly happen next.

Experience has convinced us that the best way to enjoy a pool—is to move next to the fella who owns one.

Love,
Char

LETTER FORTY-FIVE

Dear Lennie,

. . . I've wondered just where I should put this incident. Since I have it filed under "bloopers," I guess it would fit in quite naturally after the swimming pool fiasco. When you've read it, you may wonder why I've included it at all. But I included it because I believe there is great therapeutic value in a hearty laugh!

This all happened just after you moved, back when I only had three children—and very small ones at that.

The pastor called and said, "Char, we have a lady missionary in town. We weren't expecting her until the weekend. Could you put her up for the night? She's a single girl—a real dedicated one, too."

I thought of the ring in the bath-tub and the chaotic condition of the spare-room the kids had been using for a playroom, so I chirped a bit deceitfully, "Sure, that'll be fine."

Gene was in the living room enjoying his paper and an occasional peek at TV. I broke the news to him as gently as I could. (This was before the days of checking things out with your "head" before you made decisions.)

I said, "Dear? The pastor wants us to put up a lady missionary for the night—I hope you don't mind. Would you be a doll and go tidy up the bathroom while I fix the bed for her?" Then I hurried out of the room because I didn't want to hear his reaction

I took one look at the spare room. Since I believed at that time that the age of miracles was past, I decided to give her our bedroom. It was already 9:30 in the evening, and she would be here any minute. I changed the sheets and pushed what I couldn't cram into a closet under the bed and hustled downstairs to appear well organized even to the point of a pot of coffee and what few cookies I'd managed to save from the neighboring hordes of small fry.

After introductions, she and I were chatting over our coffee while Gene and the pastor were deep into some discussion about something or other. I mentioned to her that she shouldn't be surprised if one of the kids got in bed with her, as I was giving her our room—she assured me that she loved kids, and that she would understand.

About that time the pastor overheard us talking about the kids and made the comment that he couldn't get over how big the boys were getting and that they were growing like weeds. We had a bit more of such exciting talk, and then the pastor excused himself and said goodnight. And as she and I were very tired, we decided to go to bed also.

Gene? He went back to his favorite chair and his newspaper.

After I'd gotten our guest settled, I promptly died, as I have a habit of doing the minute I hit the bed—even the lumpy spare room kind.

About an hour later I was awakened by my distraught husband who was standing in the doorway, silhouetted against the moonlight coming in the window behind him—a lovely setting for his emotion-packed voice that was trying to tell me something in a stifled, high-blood-pressure kind of mellow bellow.

It seems the poor fellow went to his own bedroom the way he is accustomed to doing—praise God. Not wanting to disturb anyone, he hadn't turned on a light. He pulled the covers partially back and was about to get in when he discovered Body Opposite had both pillows. He, thinking this was a bit too much, pulled the bottom pillow out somewhat unceremoniously, and muttered something about me having lost my senses—to which a sleepy muffled voice said, "I believe you have the wrong bed." He replied, "Now cut that out! It wouldn't be so funny, y'know," as he sat on the edge of the bed.

By then Body Opposite was wide awake and informed him that he really *did* have the wrong bed, and by that time she was talking to a stream of,

"Oh, NO—so sorry—didn't know"—as he awkwardly grabbed up his clothes that were strung all over his own bedroom—stumbled over her suitcase and fell towards the door.

By the time I was aware of what had happened, he was standing there in the doorway, absolutely weak with embarrassment creaking, "Charlene Potterbaum! How *could* you! I almost went to bed with a *missionary!*"

I was torn between wild hysteria and utter despair as I realized I had never taken the time to tell my poor darling husband that I was putting the guest in OUR room—and that *we* were sleeping in the spare room!

The next morning she came down the stairs, took one look at me and said, "Well, when he started to get in bed with me I thought, 'my, her children ARE big.'" Then she went on to say, "It was just a mistake, don't feel bad. We missionary nurses are told to be prepared for anything. . . ."

And with that I thought I was going to bust a blood vessel because she hadn't even intended to be funny!

Lennie, do you see why I don't drink? I get into too much trouble *sober!*

Love,
Char

LETTER FORTY-SIX

Dear Lennie,

Phyllis called the other day and said, "Can you come over for coffee in the morning? There'll be about six here. I've invited my sis. She sure has been asking a lot of questions lately. Hope we can come up with some answers for her—she isn't a Christian, but I think she's getting "hungry.""

I said fine and that I'd be there.

The next morning we invaded Phyllis' domicile with the usual flurry that accompanies a bunch of enthusiastic women and planted ourselves at her kitchen table conspicuously near the coffee pot. We all happily began to exchange blessings we'd received from the Lord and were all talking excitedly at once—because we'd all been so blessed we almost tried to out-talk one another.

Suddenly, in the middle of the chatter, Phyllis' sister Gail began to cry. We stopped in the middle of our various suspended sentences, and since I was beside her I said, "Gail, what's wrong?"

She said, "Oh, I feel so silly—but you're all going on about how good the Lord has been to you—and—oh, I want Him, too!" and she cried all the harder.

We all joined hands, bowed our heads, and I asked Gail to repeat after me as I led her through a prayer asking for salvation. Then we all thanked the Lord together for bringing Gail into His family—and we went on happily picking up our suspended sentences and sharing with her about more of the goodness of the Lord.

Just all in a day's coffee break!

I marvel at the Holy Spirit's willingness to bear witness to a soul in need that what His children are saying is true! His power can work and pluck at a heart when we aren't even aware of it. I feel so sorry for people who think that being a Christian is a drag!

Love,
Char

LETTER FORTY-SEVEN

Dear Lennie,

I believe the Lord allows summer vacations to happen so He can test the mettle of our faith! My summer days are engulfed with hedge to hedge kids—and then there is "Peter-next-door, who came with the house."

I think every mother begins to feel the strain about the latter part of August. Especially mothers who have discovered the value of extensive prayer time, and the therapeutic wonders that can be worked in a heart through study of the Word! There just isn't that much time available amidst the demands of an active household. Yet, I know the Lord understands, because He gave me these precious kids, and He, above all, would know where my responsibilities lay . . . lie . . . lay . . . I really must brush up on my grammar.

Lennie, about the end of August I saw what I could be if I were to wrench myself loose from the Savior's love for even a moment. Although I snitched every minute with Him that I could, I still felt the draining of spiritual life. Without that close communion with Him, I saw myself "closing in on myself." By that, I mean I saw "self" coming to life and being assertive. I found my "self" demanding things that God didn't want me to have at this time. I began to see glaring flaws in others, yet I could hardly see *mine* at all. By the time August rolled around, I felt almost as though I were hanging on by a thread—but praise the Lord, it was that thread I mentioned earlier—the one that is blood-red and strong!

There was an interesting thing that happened this summer, however.

It was about three in the afternoon, and the telephone rang. I came up with a breathless "Hello," as I'd just run up from the basement.

Without any warning, an unknown voice on the other end came up with a vulgar, insidious proposition. I gasped . . .

But just ever so quickly, after I caught my breath, a verse came to me. It's in Ephesians 6:12— in the Living Bible it reads, "For we are not fighting against people made of flesh and blood, but against persons without bodies—the evil rulers of the unseen world, those mighty satanic beings and great evil princes of darkness who rule this world; and against huge numbers of wicked spirits in the spirit world."

And then quickly, the Holy Spirit said, "Come against that spirit with my love. . . ."

So I took a deep breath, steadied my shaking knees and said, "Oh, you poor thing! Don't you know that Jesus loves you and that He died for

you? Jesus loves you . . . He died for you . . ."
And then it was time for the voice on the *other*
end to gasp!

He said "Who IS this?"

And I said "What does it matter? You had a
message from your master and I have one from
mine! And His message is one of love . . . He
can help you . . . Oh, He loves you so . . ."

He made no move to hang up, and not wanting
to give the spirit that had this poor soul in its control any ground, I began softly to sing "Oh, the
blood of Jesus." (I knew the blood of Jesus and
the love of Jesus could be as repulsive to ... evil
spirit as its filth was to me!)

You see, we'd been plagued by a rash of obscene
phone calls previously. Unfortunately, the other
times my girls got the "full blast"—which upset
me quite a bit. I'd even felt hatred creep into my
heart for this terribly warped personality.

But I made the discovery that, as I was obedient
to the Lord and came against the controlling
spirit—realizing indeed that it *was* a spirit, I
could have love and compassion for the person
whom the unclean spirit was controlling. I felt the
love of God welling up within me as I spoke to
him of His love—and what a safeguard for bitter
hatred creeping into my *own* heart.

I felt quite sure he'd never call again—unless it
would be to tell me about his conversion!

Love—
Char

LETTER FORTY-EIGHT

Dear Lennie,

Wouldn't you know it? I blew it.

Just when everything was going so well, too. I muddled the whole business up by the good intentions of some learned men—and I blew it.

Things were going quite well. I'd been adhering to the things I'd been telling other young mothers, doing my best to "practice what I preached." Then I picked up an interesting book with a strong psychology flavor. The author felt it wise for couples to be honest with one another.

I agreed with that.

Then he made an interesting comment that our stomachs have a way of keeping score when others offend us in one way or another.

I agreed with that.

He then went on to talk about the different levels of communication, and that, in order to have the best communication, sometimes it is necessary to speak out the truth in love even though it might hurt the other individual.

234

I THOUGHT I agreed with that . . . but now I'm not so sure.

I shared some things from the book with Gene. I thought I'd get real communicative and share a few of the things my stomach had been keeping score of . . . on a comfortable, mature level, of course. But wouldn't you know it? His stomach had been keeping score, too . . . and before we knew it, we had some hurt feelings and misunderstandings because our emotions wouldn't let us see clearly what the other one was trying to get across.

Well, we both thought it was a big loss. We didn't feel particularly edified. It took a whole basin full of grace to heal the sore spots, but of course Jesus always comes through.

And when I was feeling twinges of condemnation, I stumbled across some more words of a wise man who said that wives *should* speak out their feelings, at times, so their mate can know where the hurt areas are. It helped to quiet the condemnation temporarily, but there was still some "dis-ease" in my spirit.

I had to call the pastor about something else, but I threw in a casual, "by the way, Gene and I got very honest with one another last night. According to what I've been reading, it was the right thing to do. So why am I so miserable?"

And then, he said the very words that confirmed what the Holy Spirit had been trying to bring to the "fore" all along in my innermost being.

He said, "I imagine you are miserable because you took the word of these authors over and above I Peter 3."

And immediately, I saw how foolish I'd been. God has made provision in His Word for all the answers to life's problems, but I had dared to believe there might be other angles, too.

So there I was—mighty counselor of women—in all my fizzled splendor. I'd tripped up on my own message! Hadn't I told young mothers that their husbands could be won "without a word?" Respectfully, I read again through I Peter, chapters two and three. (Lennie, go take a peek at them yourself—hope you've gotten an Amplified by now.)

Now, you'll see that chapter 3 starts out with a sanctified, "In like manner. . . ." I personally think the like manner he is talking about refers back to the "patient suffering" mentioned in chapter two, where Peter says in verse 20 that "if you bear patiently with suffering (which results) when you do right and that is undeserved it is acceptable and well-pleasing to God."

You see, I felt Gene had not been obeying "the Word" because he had gotten a bit more engrossed in his own interests than suited my tastes—and I felt neglected. My score-keeping tummy said, "He doesn't need a wife. Just a house-keeper, a TV, and a newspaper. That's all."

And about this time, these books came my way

236

encouraging me to "Level with him. Let him know how you feel."

So I did. And I felt it was absolutely disastrous, because I knew I'd rushed in ahead of the wisdom of God—I'd rushed in ahead of the convicting power of the Holy Spirit. I'd rushed in ahead of fervent prayer to God, asking him to nudge the heart of my husband—in short, I'd gone the world's way.

How much pleasanter it would have been if I had just simply gone before the Lord, stated my case, left it in His hands and sat back and waited for the blessed Holy Spirit to make my erring husband conscious of the fact that we were not taking the time it takes to make a marriage "work." It would have taken a bit longer, I'm sure—but I would have had the additional blessing of learning patience under quiet, planned-of-the-Lord waiting until the time was right for my prayer to be answered—His way. I would have proven the value of "what He sees in secret, He will reward openly."

And too, I'd have gained another victory in the area of "dying" to self. If I had handled this whole thing God's way, I would have been saying to God, "My hurts are not important—the only important thing is obedience to your Holy Word." And through obedience to His Word, the power of God would have been released into my situation.

Lennie, if we'd only take the time to cover the

faults in others with love, the way God intends for us to—we wouldn't have to "cover" our score-keeping tummies with antacids so often!

And of course, I still think that "speaking the truth in love" is vitally important and definitely scriptural. But there are some things God allows to come into a marriage so that long-suffering and forbearance can flourish, I'm sure.

And praise God that He gave us both a sense of humor! We get a big chuckle out of the episode now, when we mention it . . . which, you can be sure, isn't too often!

More later—
Char

LETTER FORTY-NINE

Dear Lennie,

Oh, me.

I thought this letter would be so easy to write. It seemed as though it all came to me so readily when I was praying, but here I sit wondering what it will possibly look like in black and white. I want so much for my heart to reach out and touch yours, but sometimes I'm afraid I will thrust it out and it will come shattering down into my coffee cup; and while I am picking up the pieces, we will have missed God somewhere.

I have really been under satanic attack lately as the book—our book—nears the end. Due to the fact that I am a most imperfect human being, these letters often have to be re-written and re-done. When I pick them up to re-work them a bit, and to wring out (hopefully) the last vestiges of flesh in them, old "what's-iz-name" (Satan) comes at me with, "Look at that! Nothing but 'I' this and 'I' that! Who are you trying to kid? Your starved ego is there just as blatantly as it ever was! Tear that up and forget the whole business! Who'd want to read that, anyhow!"

Now I don't relish even giving him a paragraph in one of our letters, but by the same token, God *did* mention the Philistines quite often so we could be aware of the enemy's tactics—and of how powerfully God fought the battles for the children of Israel. Therefore, let me say that the devil has given me tremendous torment in the last few weeks, but I am determined that God should receive the glory from even this, because it means that Christ is making some inward advances in my life, and in our book—OR SATAN WOULDN'T CARE SO MUCH!

Lennie, I don't mind my heart lying . . . laying . . . lying (will I ever get my grammar straight?) here for all the world to see—until I think of someone reading it who knows me well. Then I really cringe because old slew-foot gets in there with both his slew-feet and says, "How do you think so-and-so will feel when they read this? They know what you really are! They know all the times you've failed! They've seen you at close range—they know all the times you've been in the flesh! And look at you and Gene! You had a misunderstanding the other day, didn't you? You got good and mad, didn't you? He acted saintly, but you were a mess! How DARE you write a book telling others 'how to' when you've failed so!"

So, needless to say, I wouldn't even be able to

240

hold my head up, much less attempt to minister to others if it were not for the saving grace of Jesus Christ, Who loves me in spite of my failures, Who sees within me the willingness to go on in spite of falling short at every turn.

Lennie, I AM determined to go on, even though I know I have not achieved perfection, have not even begun to scratch the surface of this business called "Christian maturity." I believe that God created me for *one purpose* and *one purpose only!* And that purpose is to communicate the Love of God to a dying world! And before Satan can attack and tell me what a sickeningly pious crack that was, I want to tell you THAT IS THE REASON GOD CREATED EACH AND EVERY ONE OF US!

How I praise Him for the wonderful shield of faith He has provided. For no matter how hard Satan whips and lashes at me, that powerful shield is right in there, staving off the blows and making the battle most enriching because each lash from Satan only drives me deeper into God!

And I said, "Lord, thank you because Satan cares so much. We must be really gaining some ground, Lord. But, Lord, there *are* a lot of 'I this's' and 'I did that's' in my letters. I don't really see any way of getting around that, Lord, because these are my experiences—*our* experiences—with one another and those around us. What should I do?"

And, so tenderly, He said, "Just be still and

241

know that I am God. When you get out on thin 'I's', I'll haul you back in, Myself."

Now truly, "If God be for us . . . who can be against us?"

Love,
Char

LETTER FIFTY

Dear Lennie,

Aren't we mothers a peculiar lot? I had one come in on me the other day all torn up because "her daughter was being treated so dirty by her girl-friend." (Both age 11!) She said it hurt her so to see her daughter treated "so badly" and then go right back to being friends again within just a couple of hours.

I mean, her feathers were really ruffled.

It took me quite a few minutes to make her see that this ability to forgive was one of the beautiful traits of children . . . one I'm quite sure the Lord intended for us to imitate when he told us that "we should become like little children." In fact, I'd say it is one of the most important traits.

Yet I see grown people carrying grudges, grinding axes, getting even, talking people "down"—even Christians.

I don't think I ever realized the full meaning of the portion of scripture that says "forgive me my trespasses as I forgive those who have trespassed against me" until I became baptized in the Holy

Spirit. As we cling to some trivial hurt down here, not willing to forsake it and be cleansed from it, I believe a little bit of heaven is held back from our hearts that would otherwise come rushing in to make our life here more pleasant and blessed. Because this is really what it's all about—having a blessed journey—not only that ultimate goal. I may have a mansion in glory, but I'd also like to have glory in my mansion down here.

Love,
Char.

LETTER FIFTY-ONE

Dear Lennie,

Never having had any training in "book writing" I'm at a complete loss as to how you end one! Guess I will have to take my publisher's request of only so many pages as some kind of cue to wind this up. And then it will be difficult, because stopping almost anywhere would be like stopping in the middle of a sentence—the life sentence I am committed to—of telling of His wondrous works to the children of men.

It seems such a short time ago when I was "commissioned" by the Lord to write for Him through Bryn, a brother in Christ from Wales. Thanks to the Lord's provision of another free trip, we were whizzing through the countryside of Wales. I was so taken by the fantastic scenery, I could hardly keep my mind on the conversation, until I realized the Lord was really trying to speak to me through this brother. The small foreign car was loaded with people and luggage, so our conversation was threaded through the brass handle of a monstrous suitcase that separated us.

As we had a five hour drive ahead of us, I began telling him of some of the things I've shared here in these letters. Quietly, he said, "Sister, I believe the Lord would have you put this into writing. There are many men who are writing about their walk in the Spirit—I think it is time we hear from our women, and what the Lord is doing in their lives. I'm going to be praying that you will consider this. I don't want to hear any talk about lack of confidence in your ability. God's people need to be centering their confidence on His ability to do wondrous things through His vessels, in spite of their imperfections. It has nothing to do with self-confidence, but all to do with Christ confidence."

This came as a welcome word as I'd been sensing a rising desire within me to write for the Lord, but felt everything that needed to be said had already been said elsewhere by others more learned than I. (I hadn't yet fully grasped the wonder of our uniqueness, and His uniqueness in dealing individually with us.)

So, I came back from Europe with an even keener desire to write but asking the Lord for yet more confirmation. We arrived home on Saturday, and on Sunday the first prophecy was aimed directly to my innermost being when a dear saint (someone I respect and love very much—but who hadn't been there for some time, and didn't even know we'd been to Wales), stood up right behind me and said, "The work that I have given thee to do—see thou do it. Thus saith the Lord."

I wept like a baby!

And you scoffers of prophecy better watch your scoffing, because I Thessalonians 5 warns "not to despise prophesyings." And if that wasn't enough, the second prophecy came through a brother who said, "The love that I have shed abroad in your hearts is to be shed abroad into the hearts of others." (This was almost word for word the very thing I had asked God to permit me to do only a few days previously.)

Coincidental, you say? No wonder your experience is lifeless! To me, it was direct confirmation that He had truly commissioned me, and this book is evidence that *He meant what He said!* I had only to be obedient to the vision He had set before me.

The next thing I had to face was Satanic onslaught. It went like this: "Who'd read that drivel . . . that's sickeningly pious. . . ." And when I sent the partial manuscript off to publishers, a sneering voice would say, "So what . . . if someone takes it, you won't be able to finish it . . . you'll never think of anything else to add to it . . . remember the teacher who said she thought you could write but that *you'd probably never write a book?* You've started something you can't finish . . . you're going to make a fool out of yourself . . ."

Another line of attack—and perhaps the one that gave me the biggest hassle was the one about, "But you're a WOMAN! Women aren't supposed to put themselves forth! They are to be quiet . . . you shouldn't be stepping out like this. . . ."

And now that I think about it, isn't his line of attack two-faced? I mean, on the one hand he was trying to discourage me from stepping out to share the wonders of God's dealing in our lives. Yet, on the other hand, he is knocking himself out to proclaim women's rights through women's libbers—how they are equal to men, how they should stand up for their own rights, etc.!

Well, praise God, I learned to live with that sneering voice—indeed, even began to gauge my success by how loud and sneering the voice was! The more he tried to tell me the book was no good, the more expectant I became that it might be good since his whole nature is one of lying!

The next snag I had to overcome was put before me by a well-meaning saint who made the comment that he "never read anything but the Bible." It really put me in a turmoil. If everything we needed to know was in that one precious Book, why should I clutter up bookshelves with another one?

Again, I went to the Lord.

And seeing the need of my heart, He caused me to think about that scene beside the Sea of Galilee where He fed the multitudes. I visualized Him taking the loaves and giving thanks. Then I saw Him handing the broken loaves to His disciples, who then gave it to the multitudes. But He had me pay special attention to the "broken meat that was left." (Many times I'd wondered what these broken pieces meant.)

He seemed to almost be saying to me, "What do those broken pieces mean to you?"

And, being basically conservative, I said, "left-overs."

"And what do left-overs mean to you?"

I thought a moment. "Something with nutritional value if served properly with just the right amount of domestic ingenuity and spice to bring out the flavor."

And then I saw what He was trying to say! The ministers of His Word are those He has raised up to break the Word for us—but there would always be bits and pieces—sharing, testimonies, experiences—that could be used to take people by the hand and lead them to the stronger "meat."

As a confirmation to my revelation, I ran across this gem from the preface to *What Shall This Man Do?* by Watchman Nee.

He says, "We humans are not to produce perfect books . . . if God gives us books they will ever be broken fragments, not always clear or consistent or logical, lacking conclusions, and yet coming to us in life and ministering life to us."

That is, and has always been my prayer concerning these "fragments" of my life and walk in the Spirit—that they might minister life—and joy—and peace—to our readers, those who have peeked over our shoulders.

And so, with this in mind I bid you a tender

goodbye, dearest Lennie. I think I read somewhere that "good-bye" is an old English derivative of "God be with you. . . ." So what could be more appropriate?

I can only pray that this book will somehow make its way into your life—that someone, somewhere will know of a Lennie Gill who once lived to the west of my kitchen window. And daily, as I write these letters to you, I pray that God is making your heart hungry for more of Him—and that you have not experienced tragedy, that Satan has not tried to rip your marriage apart as he has so many others; that that tremendous personality of yours has not been warped by vanity or damaged by bitterness.

Have you thought much about Jesus, Lennie?

He has thought much about you . . .

In Christian Love,

Charlene—your kookie neighbor to the east of your kitchen window

12-74

ACKNOWLEDGMENTS

This manuscript could never have been presented to my publishers in a legible manner had it not been for the devoted typing of Mrs. Judy Gilbert, Miss Harriet Schrock, and my niece, Mrs. Jim McGee.

A heartfelt Thank You to Anita Bourbon and Judy Gilbert for their constructive criticism. They knew it might damage my ego, but never our friendship!

An especially warm, loving, tender thanks to my dear husband and family who went without cakes and cookies so I could finish this book.

A big thank you to my pastor, Vic . . . and to his flock for keeping me in line. . . .

But most of all, I extend a grateful heart heavenward to a Holy God Who saw the desire to write, and caused that desire to be met. Thank you, Jesus.

WHEREVER PAPERBACKS ARE SOLD
OR USE THIS COUPON

 Whitaker House

504 LAUREL DRIVE
MONROEVILLE, PA 15146

SEND INSPIRATIONAL BOOKS
LISTED BELOW

Title	Price	Send Complete Catalog
_____	_____	
_____	_____	
_____	_____	
_____	_____	
_____	_____	
_____	_____	
_____	_____	
_____	_____	

Name_____

Street_____

City_____State_____Zip_____